sequence

a mixtape of writings

editor
Jon Miller

associate editors
Holly Baker
Kate Tasseff
Scott Kenimond
Sean Miller

ISBN 978-1-62922-079-6

Manufactured in the United States of America.

sequence
a mixtape of writings

Side A

Side B

side A

Trapped
Hannah Adams

Caroline sighed as she placed the book back into its place amongst the tall rows of shelves. She let her eyes wander along the titles, searching for what to read next. It seemed she had read almost all that had interested her at this point.

She had to wait at the library near her mother's work every day after school, since the bus didn't go far enough to drop her off at home. She asked her mom why she couldn't just go to the school near her house, but her mother insisted that "this school was better for her" and "gave her more opportunity." She appreciated the sentiment but didn't understand why her mom was so against their old middle-class life. Sure, they were on the lower end of the middle class and struggled to get by at times, but it was still nothing to be ashamed of. Her mother has been like that ever since she got the new job after the divorce.

Caroline huffed quietly thinking about it but continued to look for a new book to distract herself. She went to the back wall, letting her fingers glide along the spines of the books, so she could focus on the various titles better. *She* stopped at a shelf when she felt a cool breeze hit her palm.

That's odd. She thought to herself. I've never noticed this draft before.

She then looked between the two shelves and just as she suspected there was a slight view of an opening. She turned back, looking around to be sure no one could see her, before grabbing the side of the shelf and tugging. It was heavy, but with enough effort she had just the amount of strength to pull it forward slightly. She tugged again and cringed as the wood scraped against the floor with an ear-splitting screech. She paused making sure she didn't alert anyone before giving it one last tug. She heard a book fall through the back of the shelf and tumble down the opening.

Great. She thought. *I was just gonna take a peek, but I suppose now I have to go get that.*

She squeezed herself through between the shelves and made her way into the opening. It was dark, but luckily, she was able to see the top step of the staircase that led down.

A basement? But why would they block it off?

She stepped down letting her hand glide along the wall to steady her as she descended. She carefully stepped down for a while till she finally saw a crack of light below. When she reached it, she realized it was a door. She felt around for the knob before opening it.

What the Hell?

When she opened the door, she was met with what appeared to be outside. A forest with a blue sky and the sound of chirping birds.

I must be dreaming...

Just as she thought that her foot hit something on the floor, kicking it into the grass beyond the door. She stepped forward and picked it up. It was the book.

The Complete Field Guide to Your New Adventure

I've never seen this book before. This is starting to freak me out.

She decided she was just gonna go back, but when she turned around the door was gone. No door, no staircase, nothing.

She was trapped.

Blizzard
Natalie Savage

Emily huddled inside a cocoon of blankets, shivering even as she sat inches from the fireplace. The wind howled outside, and a glance to the window revealed a swirling, white cloud set upon a black backdrop. The door of her chalet rattled on its hinges, causing her to jump.

She inched closer to the fireplace, taking care to avoid dragging the fleece blankets into the flames. The teacup gripped in her hands did little more to warm her than the fire did.

Cold, tired, and full of worry, she cursed everything from the snow to the mountain to her husband, who had foolishly—he considered it bravely—left their chalet earlier in the afternoon to help the old lady further down gather more firewood. His kind heart was one of the many reasons she loved him, but not so much when he was aware the mountain would be engulfed in a blizzard the same day.

"I'll be back in time," Emily groused under her breath, trying to assuage her worry. "The blizzard couldn't possibly come early, now could it?"

But with every second her husband remained out her worry grew. What if he got lost again? What if he was attacked by wolves? What if he fell into a ditch somewhere and broke a bone? What if he fell off the *mountain*?

And that did it. Emily kicked off her blankets, bundled up in her thickest snowsuit, and grabbed a sled from the attic along with the thickest rope she could find. "We are both idiots," she muttered. "Absolute, complete, and utter idiots."

She opened the door, groaning as a wall of snow collapsed inward all over her mother's favorite rug. She squinted out into the darkness, reaching for one of her ski poles. Using it as a sight cane, she carefully waded out into the curtain of white.

"Richard!" she screamed, but she could barely hear herself over the gusts of icy wind. "Richard!" She could hear nothing but the wind, and her heart thumped painfully in despair. He could be laying prone two feet from her, and she would never see or hear him.

Gathering her courage, she continued feeling her way down the path, tears of terror freezing to her cheeks. "Rich—"

Something grabbed her ski pole and her call for her husband turned to a wordless shriek. She kneeled in the snow, reaching for the blackness near her pole.

Her fingers were met with cold, wet fabric and her heart leapt for joy when Richard let go of her pole, icy fingers clutching her hand. But then her joy evaporated as she could feel his groan, and she realized how weak his grip truly was. She practically tore the sled off her back and helped her husband pull himself onto it. She tied the rope around him for good measure and began to pull him back to their chalet, screaming from the exertion of pulling him up the snowy mountain.

She slipped, screaming as the sled slid away from her down the mountain path. She lunged to grab ahold of the rope again. Her body was drenched in snow and sweat alike, but she could only feel the rough texture of the rope in her hand. She pulled the sled to her and, after a couple of tries, forced herself to her feet.

She recalled the myth that Sisyphus was forced by the Greek god Zeus to push a boulder up a hill for eternity. A hysterical chuckle burst through her frozen lips that she felt rather than heard. She had wondered what would have happened if Sisyphus had refused. What if he had simply stood with the boulder at the bottom of the hill, unwilling to amuse the gods by performing such a mad task? And that was no mountain, only a hill.

The only motivation she had needed was the thought of her husband forsaken to the blizzard, freezing and groaning with no one able to hear him, while she huddled in front of the fireplace. So, like Sisyphus, every time the sled slipped from her fingers, she dove to stop it, and started over. Her face burned from the cold as her muscles burned from the labor she required of them, but she kept pulling.

She had never possessed the most physical strength, but with terror induced adrenaline heating her blood, she managed to do it. She had just enough energy to shove the door closed, bolt it, and pull Richard to the fireplace before she collapsed next to him.

Her husband was pale, and his skin felt like ice. His black hair was white with snow and wet as if he'd just taken a cold shower. His blue eyes were dazed, and he could barely bring his hand to cup her cheek, brushing away her tears. She hadn't noticed she'd broken into sobs.

"Em…" he croaked. His body convulsed, trying and failing to warm him even with the help of the fire. Pulling herself together, Emily tore off his drenched clothes and piled every blanket, cloth, or napkin in the house around him. She threw more logs onto the fire, thankful that Richard was the over-preparer that he was, before remembering that it was that same trait that got them into this mess. Then, when the blankets and fire weren't enough, she stripped and collapsed next to him, curling her body to his and burying her face into the crook of his neck.

Within minutes he felt warmer, and he placed a gentle kiss on her temple. "You idiot," she hissed, still on the brink of tears. He kissed her again, fingers tightening around her shoulder. She shook her head, pressing herself even closer. "You idiot."

Outside the storm raged, and she knew that neither of them would be able to leave for several days. But her husband was safe, and they would deal with that together when needed. Wrapped in Richard's arms, she felt warm for the first time that night, and they both slept.

I Ate Someone Else's Fries
Lemon

There's someone that looks like you
standing in the Starbucks line and
someone's jacket brushes my arm, but
I'm trying not to stare at a stranger.

People change and
I know it's not news,
but people change and
the barista is calling his name and
       people change,
       people change,
and our drinks are called at the same time.

I cut him off by accident,
a startled doe on the road.
I murmur an apology,
and he says nothing in response.
(People change, and my mouth feels sour.)

I haven't done anything
I'm supposed to and
someone with glasses
gets off on your floor with
chips and soda in hand and

someone else around the corner
looks like you and
someone else at the mall
looks like you and—
people change.
(But not really.)

Fading Memory of You
Lexus Thornton

You did this

                     No I didn't

I said "I love you"

              You never said "I love you"

Were you happy with me?

             I don't remember

Then what was—

             I never wanted this

But—

          So you don't remember do you?

You promised that
we would be together

            You promised that we would
            respect each other

        Was this love just a figment
        of our unreliable imagination?

The Last Car Ride
Kendra Ivery

The signs on the interstate passed by quickly. Lauren found herself hypnotized by their blurred words and colors. Anticipation was building in her stomach making the four-hour car ride seem much longer. She was traveling 85 miles per hour toward her very first semester of college. She had spent countless hours carefully selecting notebooks the color scheme for her room. She knew that this was going to be a much-needed fresh start. The car was littered with the remnants of her lunch. McDonalds cups and stray fries were strewn across her side of the car. Lowering her window, she inhaled deeply the smell of fresh air that rolled in from the farms that dotted the highway. As the late summer air blew through the car, Lauren looked across the center console at her mother. The two smiled at each other, and Lauren was sure her mom was just as excited as she was.

Evelyn counted the signs on the interstate as they passed. She chewed at her bottom lip and rhythmically tapped her fingers on the steering wheel. She knew that each passing sign meant that she was getting closer to having to say goodbye to her daughter. She and Lauren spent the past few weeks picking out twin xl bedding and wall décor. Throughout the whole experience, Evelyn couldn't help but feel a sense of melancholy. She was excited for her daughter, but she was also nervous. Evelyn herself had never gone to college. In fact, she had never left her hometown. It had been just the two of them since Lauren was born. She was excited for her daughter to embark on this new adventure, but she couldn't shake the sense of loneliness that was creeping in. The leftover McDonalds napkins flew around the car as Lauren lowered her window. Soon, the car was filled with sweet smelling summer air. Evelyn took a deep breath and smiled. She looked over the center console at Lauren who was already smiling at her. The two women took in their last moments together as Evelyn flipped on her turn signal and took the exit.

Home, A Place of Numerical Nuance
Emily Price

"How is your apartment coming along? Have you unpacked everything yet?" Mihika asked.

"Uh . . . it's coming along," I said. The heat of my French press coffee wafted up to my face as we strolled down the sidewalk. I tried to be nonchalant as I eyed the footfalls of my stilettos against the concrete. I carefully evaded the places the nearby tree roots had eaten up with cracks and crevices.

"It's on Bleakly Street, right?"

"Yeah. It's one of the loft apartments."

"Since we're so close, would you mind if I stopped by to take a quick look?"

"Yeah. Sure." I hoped she didn't sense the unease that oozed between my words. It wasn't as if I didn't want her to come. Of course, I wanted my close friend to come and see my new place. Her company would cradle me as I sorted through the mess of unopened boxes.

We walk for a few more blocks before I spot the address for my loft.

"Here we are," I said.

I leapt up the front three steps in one bound and fumbled with my keys. Mihika stepped up lightly behind me and peered over my shoulder.

"Do you got it?"

"Got it," I said. I mustered a disarming chuckle to cover the anxiety slowly wedging itself between us.

"Ok," she replied.

I pushed the door open. A set of twenty-four stairs stood between my apartment door and I. Twenty-four.

"After you," I said awkwardly.

"Um, you have the keys. After *you*."

I shifted my coffee into my other palm so I could grasp the banister.

Three. I leaped over the first two steps and planted both of my feet onto the third.

Six.

Nine.

She's staring. I feel it. I felt as if the windows of her soul opened wide, boring into me. *So what?* I have to do this. I have to. She wouldn't understand.

Twelve. Fifteen. Eighteen. Twenty-one. Twenty-four.

If Mihika said anything, I didn't hear it. I unlocked my door as soon as I could and pushed through. She followed closely behind.

"Wow, it's pretty nice in here . . . except for all the boxes. I would have thought you would have been settled in a little more. It's been about nine months since you got the apartment, right?"

"Yeah," I ran a hand through my hair and sighed, "You know, I've just been so busy with work I haven't really had the time. Um, do you want me to still show you around?"

I led her to the kitchen. By instinct, I carefully avoided the cracks in the tile and wove through the boxes with dishes haphazardly piled stacked inside.

"Nice colors," Mihika commented.

Next, I took her up to the loft. I felt a sense of déjà vu as the stairs were taken in multiples of three and I felt the weight of her concern.

As we entered the brown-sugar colored room, I could only think of the ceiling. The nights I counted the panels in hope they would promise peace and sleep. In the mornings, I had to do the same thing. I had to. If I didn't, I might not make it to work that day. I could slip down the stairs. I could get in a car crash.

I wish I counted sheep.

"It's a lovely bedroom. I'd love to see it furnished a bit, don't you think?"

I tried to avert my eyes from the panels. They reminded me too much of the fears I had to fight off this morning before getting coffee. I didn't want to return to that headspace.

"Let me help you. We can work on it together. I'm somewhat of a HGTV ambassador at this point. I watch it so often that Stephen has to turn it off when I'm not looking."

"I would like that," I said. The first authentic smile of the day played on my lips.

If I Don't Pick Up the Phone
Scott Kenimond

When you call
maybe I am sleeping
sound in silent slumber

dreaming of when you finally
fell in love with me
all those years ago.

Maybe I am sitting on the floor
of my oversized shower
water caressed, thinking

of how and why I fell so
hard for you then,
a derailing train.

Maybe I am out with a friend
occupying my dragging time
avoiding lamentable thoughts,

or looking for someone to come over
after all, we are no longer
and sex is better than reflection.

If I don't pick up the phone
when you call
maybe I am finally forgetting you.

They Can't Take That Away from Me
Kate Tasseff

The Omicron variant took my family's Christmas plans, pumped them full of lead, tossed them in a trash compactor, put the compacted plans on a pyre, drowned them in gasoline, porcupined them with a thousand off-brand trick candles, and gave them the once-over-twice with a flamethrower while a fifth grade band played the "1812 Overture" on kazoos. Relationships were stretched thin and torn. Tempers flared, and depression glommed onto shoulders like a weighted blanket with a duvet cover made of cold, damp seaweed.

But at *least* it didn't take my sense of smell.

I'm quite serious when I say that I'm not sure I could have gone on living had my smelling gone away. I come from a long line of oversensitive noses; it's a blessing and a curse. I can experience vivid time-traveling with one whiff of an old, familiar scent, but I also get crippling headaches from Bath and Body Works candles and old lady perfume. Still, the goodness is worth a little suffering now and again.

Does it make sense to you when I say that scent is emotional? Maybe it's just me. My mood flourishes when fresh mown grass rides the molecules in the breeze. The smell of inevitable rain makes me anxious. Three spritzes of Yves Saint Laurent's Black Opium on my neck raise my confidence levels by 88 percent. Garlic and butter, crock pot roast, cinnamon buns, French press coffee: tell me you aren't at least a *little* happier just imagining those within nose shot.

For me, though, the emotions that aromas cull run even closer to the heart. If I am in love with you, I am in love with your smell. I'm not talking B.O. per se, but everybody has a natural essence, and call me vampiric, but it's strongest right in the crook of your neck, and that is where I love to rest my head. A more science-y person than I might talk about pheromones, with science-y sentences like,

> Pheromones may be present in all bodily secretions but most attention has been geared toward axillary sweat which contains the odorous 16-androstenes. One of these steroidal compounds, androstadienone, is present at much higher concentrations in male sweat and can be detected by women, albeit with wide variation in sensitivity.[1]

and I would shake that science-y person's hand for making me feel like less of a psycho when I bury my nose in my couch pillow the minute my boyfriend leaves because its fabric still smells like him. I'm so far to the right of that sensitivity scale that if I pass someone in a crowd who uses the same laundry detergent he does, it makes me shiver from head to toe. If I go blind someday, like Isaac of Old Testament fame, I dearly hope no one scams me by wearing my loved one's sweaty shirts in my presence.

Anyway, since my sense of smell is still going strong post-Covid, I hope to use my powers for the good of mankind. If nothing else, I'll lend them to the Disney Imagineers, who ensure their parks' scents brainwash you into that Happiest Place on Earth mentality. Might I suggest the "bonfire bouquet?"

1. Verhaeghe, J., R. Gheysen, and P. Enzlin. "Pheromones and Their Effect on Women's Mood and Sexuality." *Facts, Views & Vision in Obstetrics, Gynaecology and Reproductive Health*, vol. 5, no. 3, 2013, pp. 189-95.

To Walk by My Side
Emily Price

"Mum didn't understand. Robbie wasn't in the picture yet…I felt like no one understood."

The *you weren't there either* wasn't uttered, but it was politely implied. Ariadne wasn't one to blame anyone. Except herself. I opened my mouth. The words were oddly featherlike and took flight.

"I'm sorry," I breathed. "I'm sorry."

Aria's knitted brows softened. She looked up at me with the eyes we shared. Well, same color but hers possessed different qualities altogether. Sharp. Piercing. *Probing.* It was as if she was finally drawn from deep thought into the present.

"It's ok, Skittles," she replied, shrugging, "You had your own friends . . . the art club and stuff. I know."

"Um," I began, my eyelashes collecting my tears, "I did."

She tilted her head ever so slightly. Inquisitive. I remembered why Mum didn't like to look her in the eyes. No one wanted you to read the pages of your story before you wrote it. Maybe *we* were the ones who shouldn't have buried so many secrets in our eyes.

I just didn't have the courage.

I traced the stitches on the quilt we stretched out on. The self-derision rose in my chest.

"I make everyone leave," I said, smiling contemptuously through the tears. "They are afraid of *me.*"

"They are afraid of your fear."

I swiped at the silent beads running down my face. "Why?"

"It makes them have to face their own."

I peered up from the quilt stitches. How did the little rambunctious, knobby-kneed sister from my childhood become the woman that I saw now? How did she become so strong?

Wasn't *I* supposed to be the strong one? I was three years older. I should have been more emotionally mature and more stalwart in my independence, right?

How did that idea fit with the comfort that my head found in the crook of her arm as I sobbed? How did it fit as she stroked my patchy hair and cradled me like a small child?

I felt the hatred that pumped in my veins slowly drain from my body. *Here* was someone who loved me so tenderly even when I abandoned her. *Here* was someone who understood me far greater than anyone could. *Here* was the friend I needed to walk me through the darkness.

"I'm here, Skyler," she said.

A Clumsy Unicyclist
Holly Baker

It was 7 a.m. when I got the last-minute call. I was holding out hope for a position at the natural history museum and I had nearly given up hope when the curator called me. He asked if I was able to make it to a noon meeting. I tried to contain the excited quiver in my voice when I said I could make the time in my busy schedule.

When preparing for any interview, I have a very important routine to build my confidence. This starts on the drive to the interview. I listen to my favorite song on repeat and rehearse the conversation out loud. I think of the most ridiculous questions so that I am prepared and all of my answers can fall from my mouth in an easy and practiced spontaneity.

So at 11:30 a.m. I began the short drive to the museum, radio quietly playing an upbeat indie song in the background. Nearly the second I opened my mouth to begin my interview, I saw him. He was dressed in a neon green suit, with pink knee pads and elbow pads, making him look like a lanky child.

His bright purple top hat was cocked lazily to one side as he struggled to find the center of balance on his unicycle. He was such an unusual sight that I nearly forgot to stop when he tipped to the right and bounced off the sidewalk toward my car. I swerved to the right and hit the brakes, coming to a stop a few feet in front of him. His palms hit my window as he used my car to keep himself from hitting the pavement. He smiled and revealed he was missing a few teeth, I had to believe from other instances like this. He let out an easy laugh and apologized.

I smiled back at him. Then he righted himself, and pedaled off, leaving me wondering what had prompted such a person to make the decisions leading to our encounter that afternoon. He had an easy confidence about him. And though he was obviously not a practiced unicyclist, his smile made me believe that he was not embarrassed by this fact.

His clumsiness actually made him endearing.

I walked into the curator's office having forgotten my pre-interview routine. Strangely, instead of the panic that should be rising from my unpreparedness, I found myself determined and confident. I walked out of the office half an hour later shaking the hand of the curator who assured me that my office would be ready by Monday.

Though I cannot be certain, I blame my success on the contagious confidence of a clumsy unicyclist.

Let's Call it an (M.) Night
Kate Tasseff

The world doesn't know how to forgive M. Night Shyamalan.

I mean, I know I don't, because he half-ruined my Valentine's Day with a real stinkbomb. But let's not get personal.

How to describe the career of M. Night Shyamalan? One could say he's like the magician who invented the "sawing a man in half" trick. He puts a man—Bruce Willis—into a big wooden box, then lifts a lumberjack-sized handsaw into the air (audiences gasp!) and begins to slice the box down the middle (audiences shriek! Bruce included!). Moments later, after hanging all in suspense, he shoves the box back together and Bruce pops out entirely intact (audiences cheer! Throw roses!) and M. Night is crowned Houdini of the Year.

The next year, he figures since that trick went like gangbusters last time, why not use Bruce Willis again, but this time, put him in a *bulletproof steel* box instead of a wooden one? Audiences are a little skeptical about the switch in material, but the trick is still fresh enough that he gets a standing ovation.

Two years later, M. Night wants to kick it up a notch. He exchanges Bruce Willis for Mel Gibson and a bunch of aliens and wraps the box in layers of tin foil. Audiences seem a bit confused, especially since Abigail Breslin is doing the sawing, but Mel Gibson in his pre-drunken-rant era, so they're still happy to see him.

Then M. Night starts getting a little too edgy. In 2006, he throws Bryce Dallas Howard in the box. She comes back for the big reveal missing her eyesight. This doesn't go over remarkably well.

In another two years, he takes the same actress, who is now *not* blind, but she *is* a mermaid, and he shoves her in a box with Paul Giamatti. No mind on earth can make this make sense. Audiences start to trickle out, cringing, one by one.

M. Night is desperate now. His magical reputation is holding on by a thread. What will turn the tide in his favor again? Who could he put under the handsaw that would bring the audiences back in droves?

That's right! Adolescents' most beloved animated TV show of the twenty-first century, *Avatar: The Last Airbender*! Only this time, he's a real boy! How could this go wrong?

Here's how: he actually saws the Avatar in half.

This, at last, is the back-breaking camel straw. M. Night flew too close to the sun and butchered a cartoon legend. For this, he now lives in the magician's equivalent of a leper colony, up to his old tricks but with a sad, distracted air, knowing they will be spit upon despite all effort.

We live in unforgiving, unforgetting times. Too bad, M. Night Shyamalan. Too bad.

Nah, I'll Wait
Sean Miller

With procrastination
I've found success,
Like a vast elation
Of drowning depth.
The magic forces
Of intuition
Come blasting forward
With mystic rhythms.
An ancient wisdom
Of prophecies old,
The faintest visions,
Forgotten and cold.
Oh, these moments, how
They're yours to savor.
So, don't do it now,
Just do it later.

Who Are You?
Tyler Shea

I never realized it was happening until I was in early college and I tried to make friends. They would ask me the classic small talk / getting to know somebody questions such as: "What is your favorite color?" or "Do you have a favorite food?" and I would realize that I didn't have answers to give. I found that I was making up the answers so that I wouldn't be embarrassed that I did not know who I was outside of the digital world.

It turns out that I seemingly lost six years of time due to disassociation, and I have yet to understand what caused me to focus so deeply on entertainment and distancing myself from reality. Something drove me to stay in the digital world whether it be through video games, YouTube, or streaming services, I would be immersed for almost nineteen hours per day if I didn't have school. It could very well have been adolescent depression or some form of trauma, but I know for sure that I abandoned myself and grew away from my own personality for years.

Only in the past few years have I come back into touch with who I am as a person and asked those introductory questions that I did not have answers for and can now come up with answers. It is taking a long time to get to know myself once again but that is what it takes to understand the one person you should understand inside and out.

Lost, Then Found
Jacob Fairfield

All I remember hearing was a loud bang before losing consciousness. When I awoke, the pod had already completed the landing process. I checked all the sensors and tried initiating a thorough scan of the area, but nothing worked. After realizing I would be on my own, I opened the pod door and was greeted by the sight of a forest canopy. In the distance, I could make out large stone pillars that had a subtle shine when the sun hit just right. The sight was breathtaking, but I knew that I couldn't stay there.

I climbed down the tree the pod had mistakenly believed to be a safe landing space, and reached the bottom layer. A thick fog covered most of the area, making it almost impossible to see. Luckily however, the sensor I pulled from the pod was still able to serve as a compass. Relieved, I began heading north towards the stone pillars, hoping that maybe I could reach an area high enough to make out something, anything that might have helped.

Trekking through the fog and the undergrowth was no easy task. I began hallucinating simple man-made structures such as a bakery on the corner of a street, or a lonely bench at a bus stop. I pulled myself together and marched forward. Eventually, I reached an opening beneath one of the enormous stone pillars. With no trees around, the sunlight began shining down and illuminated carvings in the brown stone of the pillar. I couldn't make out the markings, but it was clear someone, or something, had created these. Glancing up at the structure, I knew it would be treacherous, but I had no choice. I began to climb.

It felt like hours had gone by with little progress. The sunlight had faded away a while back, leaving my sensor as the only light source, but it wouldn't last forever. The climb itself, however, was both terrifying and exhilarating. At last, I discovered a small cave towards the top. I entered it, curious as to where it might lead. The stone that once covered the walls was replaced with what looked like drywall, and window frames covered by stone on the opposite side. It had to be a dream. The benches, the bakery, the drywall, there was no way it could be true. I searched around and discovered what looked like a marble plaque sitting against the wall. However, before I could examine it, the sensor's light died, leaving me alone in darkness. Reaching around, I hoisted up the plaque, and brought it towards the edge of the cave, where the light from the moon illuminated the drawing. At long last, I found it. Pictured was a family standing beneath a torii, one that I was sure I had seen before. As the moonlight continued to light up the area, I could see the remnants of what was once Tokyo, with what was left of Mount Fuji sitting alone in the distance. At long last, I was home again.

The Lovely Smile of Miss Étoil
John Thomas

"Mary-Ann, it's time for breakfast," Mother's voice
rings through the halls, rousing me from my slumber. I rub the sleepiness from my eyes and climb
out from under the sheets, quickly making my bed
and changing out of my nightclothes. A plain green
dress should do for the day. Nothing too boisterous
but still formal enough to not seem uncouth.

I head to the dining room, taking a seat at the
table across from Mother, a plate of steaming eggs
and toast set before me, a glass of grape juice set to
the side. "It looks delicious as always, Mother," I say
politely before taking a bite, smiling as I swallow,
before grabbing the glass of juice and taking a sip.

It's always hard to keep a smile while drinking it,
but I've practiced enough to hide my thoughts on the
bitter taste. I quickly wipe some of the liquid from
my lips with my napkin before taking another bite of
breakfast while Mother reads the morning paper.

"Are you excited for today? Your father is getting off work early to come and celebrate with us,"
Mother says sweetly, clearly excited for the coming-
of-age party she'd arranged. She'd even arranged
for the bakers to prepare a cake for the occasion. I
doubt I'll be allowed more than a slice though, any
more would be unladylike.

"Oh, of course, Mother. It all sounds delightful," I say, going to take another sip of the juice.
Mother insists it's quite healthy for a young lady. It's
easier to simply keep her happy.

"It will be. I remember when I first came of age.
Such a delightful day. So many young men eager
for my hand. Ah, it was enough to make a maiden

blush," Mother replies, smiling at the memory as she takes another bite of her breakfast. "Oh, you simply must look your best for it. I'll have Victoria help tidy you up," she beams, positively delighted with herself. I'll likely be attending the party in a gaudy mess of ribbons.

I smile, nodding as I take another bite. "Oh, yes, I'm sure she'll help me look positively wonderful," I say, going to finish my juice, maintaining my straight face. A lady looks her best with a smile.

"Oh, of course. If I didn't trust her sense of style I wouldn't let her assist, now would I?" Mother replies, finishing her breakfast and getting up to go prepare herself for the day. I finished my food not long after, Victoria quickly arriving to take my plate, carrying it off to the kitchen to be cleaned before leading me back to my room.

"Oh, young miss Étoil, this simply won't do," she says, lifting my arm as she examines my dress. "I'm sure you have something more appropriate for such an occasion in your closet," she says, turning to step into my closet, looking around for something else. I don't know why she needs to look so hard. She helped pick out everything in there, and then organized it all by color.

She steps out carrying a light pink dress with a purple trim, a large bow on the collar that would scratch against my neck whenever I turned my head. "Oh, yes, of course, it's so lovely. I don't know why I didn't think of wearing it," I say, smiling and laughing. "Whatever would I do without you, Victoria?"

"Oh, you'd look quite silly whenever you went out, wouldn't you?" she replies, bringing the dress over. "We simply must get it on you immediately. It would be a shame if it didn't fit anymore," she says, proceeding to help me change out of my lovely green dress and into the new one she'd chosen for me. It's a bit tight around my chest and waist.

"Oh, it fits perfectly. Isn't that wonderful, Victoria?" I say sweetly, giving her a smile. Perhaps if I find a man tonight and move in with him I'll never need to wear this again. I turn my head to the side to look at myself in the mirror. The combination of colors is foul, and the bow still scratches at my neck. At least it doesn't leave a mark. But still, I smile.

The rest of the day passes similarly, Victoria helping me with makeup and jewelry until shortly before the party begins. The orchestra is set up in the ballroom, getting in the last few minutes of practice before the guests begin to arrive. I can barely hear the front door open over the sound.

"Ah, welcome home Father," I say, rushing to the foyer, offering him a curtsy.

"Mary-Ann. You look lovely," he says kindly, giving me a pat on the head. "Are you ready for tonight?" he asks, smiling warmly to me. His eyes seem to be watering a bit. Is he… going to miss me? I barely know him.

"Oh, of course Father. A girl only comes of age once, you know," I repeat the phrase Victoria had ad-nauseum as she helped prepare me.

"I know, I know," he chuckles, starting towards the ballroom. "Guests will be arriving soon. I'm going to go check on your mother. You can greet them, correct?"

"Of course Father. Victoria reviewed all my party manners today," I say, curtsying again as he leaves, not bothering to reply.

I'm not waiting long in the foyer for guests, a small family from a province to the east is the first to arrive. I believe their head of house is a jeweler, but it really doesn't matter much. I lead them to the ballroom, and Victoria goes to the foyer to greet the rest of the guests.

The party passes dully, moving from family to family, introduced to son after son, each with barely anything different to say. Listening to the script on repeat is grating. 'I'm Silverre, my father's a tailor, you're such a lovely maiden, may I have this dance?' All the names and occupations are interchangeable. Wasn't this supposed to be a wonderful night?

"Hmm… This party is rather dull, wouldn't you say?" Peter, son of a politician, who thinks I'm a lovely maiden, and has been dancing with me, asks.

"Oh, it's a rather lovely party I would say. Everyone is so kind, and the band is truly amazing, aren't they?" I reply. I must be the most respectable lady I can.

The answer elicits a groan from Peter, starting to lead me toward the side door of the ballroom while still dancing. "Oh, come now. Surely you aren't so naive. Why don't we find somewhere more private," he says, raising an eyebrow as we break off from the crowd.

"Uh… Alright," I agree, slipping out the side door with him, following his lead, giving a brief tour of some of the other rooms we passed. Eventually we reached the end of the hall, and the door to the basement. "Uh, I'm not supposed to go down there. Mother says it's not a place for a proper maiden," I explain as he opens the door, looking down the musty stairs. There's a light on down below. Odd.

"Aren't you curious then? What's being hidden from you?" he asks, a wolfish grin slipping across his face as he takes me by the wrist, leading me down the stairs.

"Oh, we really shouldn't though . . . ." I protest meekly as he leads me down to the bottom. The sight of the room is certainly astonishing. It seems to be some sort of lab. Like something maintained by an alchemist, lots of liquids being distilled, cooked, purified. Beakers and vials and papers were scattered about tables. What was being worked on here? I slowly start toward one of the tables, shouting as I suddenly feel a hand on my wrist.

"Oh, Mary-Ann, were you not enjoying the party?" Mother asks, a porcelain smile staring down at me, stepping between me and the table. "Such a shame, such a shame," she tuts, shaking her head. "And the young Peter Bougie is with you, isn't that nice?" she continues, looking him over.

"I'm sorry Mother. He wanted to see the basement," I say quietly, feeling the blood rushing to my cheeks, the red only somewhat visible beneath the layers of makeup Victoria had caked on.

"Oh, it's fine, it's fine. In fact, the two of you are just in time," Mother says as the door to the stairwell slams shut, followed by a thud. I turn, and Peter is laying in a lump on the floor, Father standing behind him. He still seemed to be breathing, but what had Father done to him?

I feel the words catch in my throat as Mother leads me over to a chair pushed up to a table in the center of the room. It's covered in golden letters in a language I don't understand, two glasses set in the center, a thick purple liquid filling them. *Grape juice.*

"Drink up, Mary-Ann," Mother says, taking a seat across from me, taking a sip from a glass of something clear but very fizzy looking. I can feel tears welling up in my eyes as I reach across the table, taking the glass and putting it up against my lips, letting the bitter taste fill my mouth. It's foul, and I can't even force a smile anymore. I wince, letting the tears stain my cheeks and wash away my makeup as I drink it down.

My vision goes blurry as I finish the glass, my body going limp. I think I fall out of the chair, but I'm not sure. My memory is cloudy. Time passes like a dream.

I can see, but when I awaken in my bed, my body isn't my own anymore, and laying next to me is Peter Bougie, but he doesn't act the way he did the night before. The way he smiles and speaks is different. It reminds me of Father.

"You look lovely, dearest," I hear my voice, but I wasn't trying to speak. My hand caresses his face, but I wasn't trying to move. Isn't 'dearest' what Mother always called Father? I try to pull my hand away, but it doesn't move.

"You've not looked more beautiful in the last 300 years, darling," Peter's body responds, smiling as he leans in, pressing a kiss against my nose. That's what Father always called Mother too, 'Darling.' I can feel my consciousness start to fade again as I start to rise from the covers, not sure if I'd be waking up again. If it would even be worth it to wake up again, if this is what life is.

The Hunt
Scott Kenimond

After I found the first one, I knew it would be a
matter of time before I located the second and
the third. "I hate looking for things," I thought to
myself, "especially when I am timed." Finding the
fourth one was a bit tricky for me as it was perched
about four feet off the ground, on the first branch
of a lazy oak tree. I was able to knock it down by
jumping up and hitting it with a stick, though this
took time as I have horrible hand-eye coordination.

With over half the time on the clock gone, I
had to pick up the pace. Moving faster and not paying attention, I stumbled upon the sixth one. I literally tripped on it. When I hit the ground, my eyes
saw the seventh just out of arms reach. I grabbed
and clawed at the earth to pull myself toward it. Just
as my hand was close enough, I grabbed hold of it.

The one-minute warning sounded. At this
point I jumped to my feet. I searched high. I
searched low. With just one minute left, I had to
find just a few more. I ran past what would be my
eighth find several times before spotting it out of
the corner of my eye. I quickly turned to grab it as
the buzzer signified the end of the activity.

Taking my findings to the front, each one was
counted and opened. In the end, I lost, finding only
eight easter eggs. I don't recall who came in first
because I was dusting the dirt off my jeans and
thinking to myself how ready I was to start counting
the bottles of beer I was about to drink.

Lavender Italian Soda
Lemon .

"Are you gonna make love to it?"
"No, but I'll let it make love to me."

The ice rendered the whipped cream tasteless
            (useless).
I won't make that mistake again.

Your affections are scattered throughout—
they battle each other, ramming
their little heads against each other,
until they're cracked and altered
            (changed, damaged).

They don't stop, they
butt those round, round skulls
over and over and—
surely they'll die.
(They never do.)

██, Down, Down
Arial DeGroff

I want it on record
that I simply desired to
...hug? Yeah, hug the floor.
The lonely, boring beige
splattered with reds floor needed
a hug that it didn't know about.
Not my fault for adding my own
contribution of reds for a good deed...

                              Not really, though.
                    I simply wanted to escape
                    reality dragging me back
              to the table where the first
              course meal was their fist.
        Over and over and over and over and-

Well, you get the idea.
So how are you?
Is the homophobic monkey cackling
too loud to generate a generic response?
        No? Then maybe it's Xanax puking
        her guts out to a hard Mike
        that just wants to get laid.
Either that or the mice have started
plotting world domination,
but only against the cat abusing
poor friend bird.

Still no?
        ...Hello?
              ...Anyone there?
                    Why can't you answer me?

Is it because I'm becoming boorish?
You can tell me.
I won't take offense.

You see, when you fall this far,
nothing else really matters.
Not the burgundy carnations drowning
optimistic sunflowers for the millionth time.
Not the devil eating away the remaining
mold mother-clock clings to her bosom.
Not the funny sparking chair
waving like an old friend as I pray
that my new home will be way far

███,

Down,

Down.

Softness as a Crime and Death as a Lover
Lemon

All the softness of the world:
without you, what would I enjoy?
Sweet, sweet sadness—
it slips between my hands.

Touch my cheek;
let me soften my pain—
magnify that it is dying
      with an angel's wing.

Cool my heart.
I want, I loved
the wind against my face.

Also known as a poet,
here you can sample
      life, love, and death
in their original translation.

Formally care but—
write poetry.

Deaths of lovers—
Early losses create poetry.

(Focus on Death.)

Old Picture
Arial DeGroff

The bright orange burn of a cigarette
bud bouncing across the granite sea
      long lost,
            long forgotten.
Blue lilies guard the home from stray cats and dogs
despite all wishes to reunite with decaying irises.
      You've never failed to sneak past, though.
         The stench of burgundy
         carnations follow you.
The routine never changes as low hums of gibberish
infest important gossip of blue jay cheating with
robin.
      Not that it matters.
         His wife died years ago.

Could you find a picture for me?
The one that captured two stupid kids
      too young,
         too smitten
in the bed of roses to be aware of poisonous thorns
digging home into her marrow,
      leaving him unprepared.
         Possibilities suffocated their fears.
Nothing could stop the inescapable leech, nibbling
her nervous smile as the downfall stains shaking
hands,
memorizing how to connect uncovered freckles
to her eyes one last time.
      Could you dust off that memory for me?
         Could you remember us this way?

Working in a Bookstore
Anonymous

Reading is one of my favorite hobbies. I can recall many summer days during my childhood spent browsing the shelves in Barnes and Noble. Most of the books I read, I borrowed from the library. But still, I loved the co-mingled smell of books and coffee. The scent combined with the low jazz music created the perfect ambiance. Finding the perfect big, cozy chair near the window often made for an afternoon full of reading.

As I got older, I began thinking about a part-time job that would interest me. I was about 17 years old and having a job was a requirement of my Marketing 101 class. I settled working for a whole-sale grocery store in the freezer department. This grocery store was located relatively close to Barnes and Noble and each commute to work had me wishing that I worked there instead.

Many years later I noticed that Barnes and Noble was in the process of hiring. I reasoned that it wouldn't hurt to dust off my resume and apply. I was called in for what would be a group interview a few days later. I had never done a group interview before, so I didn't know what to expect. It turned out to be what I'm positive is the most unique interview experience I would ever have. The answers some of the candidates gave to the store managers' questions surprised me. But the entire process reminded me of one important thing. Readers are the best and weirdest people on the planet.

The position of Bookseller is much different than I imagined it would be. I pictured getting to chat with customers about books and recommending to them some of my favorites. The reality is much different. Typically, when customers come into the store, they know exactly what they're looking for. Almost. Bleary-eyed kids and frazzled-looking parents would approach the customer service desk with their school's reading list. The kids' eyes are always glued to their phones. The parents are always in a hurry and are baffled that we are sold out of the one book that every ninth grader in the school district needs to have for the next morning. Supporters of celebrity book clubs trickle in once a month to deliver the lines, "Um, I think the cover was blue? The authors' name definitely had a letter T in it." I have perfected the art of finding these elusive books whose covers are, in fact, not blue. I can typically soothe a parent's nerves by offering free shipping to their homes. But the idea that my bookstore customers had a general disinterest in actual books threw me for a loop.

Still, there are the customers that make the job special. There are regular customers who are homebound and call every few weeks to order the next several books in their cozy mystery series. We always have fun chatting about their grandkids and the recipes in the newest Joanne Fluke novel. I've also seen an influx of young readers in search of the latest BookTok sensation. What I've learned from working in a bookstore is that readers are the most unique combination of people you'll ever come across. There tends to be tension between indie bookstores and Barnes and Noble. Additionally, many still blame us for the closing of Borders. But, with Amazon becoming a threat to all brick-and-mortar businesses and bookstores, in particular, I hope B&N will be around for decades to come.

Moon's Guidance
Sean Miller

I cannot seem to find my way,

A shade obscures the light of day.

A conjuration of the mind

Or daft inertia biding time.

To see the sky fill up with rain

And watch the moon both wax and wane,

A sentiment of sorrow lies

Within this fragile heart of mine.

In tears I burst, not from the pain,

I fear the worst will bind my chains.

The fractured fragments leave behind

A cell to keep my thoughts confined.

Although these ruminations plague

The weary workings of my brain,

I mustn't let the stars collide.

It's best when Moon and Mars align.

Just as Beautiful
Hannah Adams

The apple rolled off his desk, but he quickly caught it before it hit the tiled floor. He sighed, putting it into place again before looking back to his notebook. All he had written was the date in the top right corner.

April 29, 2022

After staring at the practically empty page for a few more minutes he sighed again, later this time and flipped back through the lined paper back to the beginning. There was his first entry, also dated.

December 6, 1928

This wasn't his first notebook, and this wasn't his first life. He let his eyes stop on the first line of the entry.

I met her again today . . . She's just as beautiful as I remembered.

Her... His love. He met her many lifetimes ago, in his first, the first he could remember at least... He met her every lifetime, same name, practically the same face, and in every lifetime, she did not remember him. He often wondered why he was able to remember his past lifetimes, but she was not. Still, in every lifetime they fell in love. Destiny. Maybe, that's all he knew to call it at least . . .

He met her again today . . . No, not her, not exactly. He met *him*. Same name, practically the same face, but him . . .

Confusing could not begin to explain how the encounter had been. In most ways it was the same as any other meeting in any other lifetime, but it was also different.

Did he feel the same love? Would he be able to make him feel the same love?

He flipped back to the new page, the apple almost fell again, this time he caught it midroll. The same action played out in a different way, but the red fruit's fate was still saved . . .

He positioned the pen on the first line.

I met my love again today... He's just as beautiful as I remembered.

Someday
Lexus Thornton

Cold days
Cold rain
Spring has appeared once again
The pastel petals flutter in the air
As the cold winter winds disappear
Gray clouds no more
Vivid colors galore
No more masks
No more fear
This is where we'll meet again
So, I hope you'll say "Hi, my friend. How have you
been?"
Just like time had never fled from our hands

All's Well that Ends Well
Holly Baker

Dear Sir,

Forgive me for the unusual format this letter takes, the bottle is necessary to give it any hope of reaching you. I do believe this hill leads to town and if my trajectory is right it should land in the back-yard of the old church yard where you used to walk daily. I sincerely hope this is still the case after these ten years.

Surely you remember that quaint little robbery that made us such close friends. I remembered it recently and decided to visit our little stash to make sure that such a large sum was still secure. I know we promised ourselves we would not do this without the other, but I was thinking only of the welfare of our financial security. I am sure you understand.

Our marker was difficult to find. I remember it just past the old graveyard wall but it took quite a bit of searching to find the correct pile of stones. Well my friend, in my desperate need to ensure your financial welfare, I found stones but it was not a wall. The well that guarded our treasure now holds the treasure that is your friend, Bruno. If you find this letter please come to the old well with a rope. I trust you remember where it is.

Counting
Lexus Thornton

Life was supposed to be enjoyable . . .
Or so I thought.
Until I realized that everything comes with a price.
The things I wanted: Money
Having fun or enough sleep: Time
It's suffocating to not have freedom
Not being able to do most things
because of the cost.
Counting sheep seems easier
than counting how much you have to let go
to play your next bill on time.

The Mood of Water
Tyler Shea

Water is the moodiest of the elements,
It constantly changes depending on the day.

One day it might embody rage
As it dashes itself upon the shore or drowns crops.

On another day it might embody melancholy,
As it makes the day dreary with a thick fog or rain.

It could also bring a joyous mood to the day,
By bringing out the beauty of the world it inhabits.

Mood is the specialty of water,
As it constantly shifts just like the current.

Maple County
Tyler Shea

The man that told me on the news
to lock my doors and windows
is not the same as I remember.

They warned us
that people were being replaced,
but I didn't believe it.

Now, here I sit,
with family that isn't family
trying to break down my door,

in an attempt to replace me.

Lunar Cravings
Emily Price

"What did you see when you stood by the brook in Hindley's Field?"

"The pool of water was still. Oddly still. I have walked those woods since I was a child, and I have never seen such quiet. On its surface, the moon reflected so peaceably—"

"Was there anything else you saw?"

"I stared at the water for some time. It felt as though if I touched it, I could fall right through. I would awake to a different world. A different life. I was so immersed that I hadn't realized the fog that swept over the earth like a cloud. It was so peculiar that I—"

"Ms. Graham, we are inquiring about a missing person's case, not your moonlight meditations. What did you see besides the brook last Monday in Hindley's Field?"

I felt the concave rings that line my eyes with my index finger and thumb. Lately, they seemed to deepen and darken so that my eyes were like two bluish lights shining through hollowed out caves.

"I saw a figure, I think," the words trickled out slow, contrasting my trancelike cascade from moments before. "The figure of a woman."

"Could you see any defining features? Hair, height, or . . ."

"She was petite, I think," I began, trying to let the words take a life of their own. "She wore a white top, and her hair was dark and coily."

The female officer nodded, "Is that all?"

"That's all."

"Thank you, Ms. Grahame. That is all the questions that we have for you. Let me lead you out to the front desk."

"Ok."

The officer placed her notes in a manilla folder and stood up to take me outside the cramped room.

"We will contact you if we need more information," she stated as we entered the hallway.

"Of course," I said.

"What was that?"

"I am willing to help in any way that I can."

The words felt foreign on my tongue. It felt as though I had shouted when, in reality, they were spoken lowly like a whisper.

"Thanks again, Ms. Grahame." The officer opened the door that led me to the front desk. "Oh —and be careful in Hindley's Field. With all this stuff happening recently, it wouldn't be prudent to take any midnight strolls. I am appreciative of your being there at the right time to help with this case. However, as someone who encounters the strange things that happen there, I have to discourage you from going there alone."

"Yes. Of course. Bye now."

Friends With a Lonely Feeling
Emily Price

I'm going out.

I imagined she said it. I imagined that she let me know. I just imagined she recognized I existed.

She didn't.

It didn't matter if she did anyway.

She threw her wallet and debit card into her baby-blue bucket bag. She swiped her keys off of her desk and switched the lights off.

I wondered where she went. I imagined that her friends probably came round the front of Apollo Commons, playfully calling out her name from the car window.

"Ju! There you are. You're going to make us late. Get in!"

I never knew, but I could assume.

I opened my laptop. Its brightness broke the darkness and stung my strained eyes. I resumed the episode of *Mork and Mindy* that I started before taking a homework break.

The show's plot swallowed me into its little world. The thing was, being out of place didn't mean you were always alone, right?

Ju and I coexisted at best, but there was a sweet start of something that I wish I could get back.

I couldn't.

It was gone with the boxes we began with but threw out as routines developed. There were no more earnest introductions into the college experience. No more of the:

"Hi, I'm Nora."

"Hey, I'm Ju! Do you need any help carrying your stuff into our apartment?'

I just became just another body to fill the room and pay half the rent. Being diligent about making my payments on time and not being a bother seemed to only punish me. There was no reason to talk and no reason to have to confront each other.

I became less than a person and more of a picture on a wall. I became a thing to think about but never someone to call.

I wish I could make other friends. I shouldn't expect to find everything in a roommate, but was it wrong for me to play out the "first friends" scenario that my favorite media taught me? Was it wrong to assume that it was how real relationships were carried out in real life?

Why did reality feel more like sitting back and watching a world I could never be a part of?

The Town Buzz
Holly Baker

The town square is the liveliest place in Arrowfield. Modeled in an Italian way, it is filled with cafés, benches, and ice cream shops. It is the kind of place where one can have a glass of wine with a friend, and watch the people go about their business.

I was enjoying my first sip of chardonnay when my lunch companion, Anna, pointed out Wilma Fret. Wilma was leaning into the ear of a poor woman who had made the unwise decision to sit next to her on the bench near the ice cream shop. Wilma's buzzing voice could be heard at our table and she twitched with the excitement of new gossip. When the woman found a pause long enough to make her excuses, Wilma hovered near the garden, waiting for another victim to sting with her sharp tongue.

"No doubt she has heard the butcher's daughter is pregnant." Anna said.

"Pregnant!" I cried. "But she is just a girl!"

"Oh yes," Anna continued, "she was hanging around with that tall skinny boy. The one that carries the walking stick everywhere. What is his name?"

"Ed." I said, confidently.

We returned to watching the neighborhood just in time to see Jacob, who owned the ice cream shop, run into the square chasing a small boy. Jacob held a rolled-up newspaper over his head like a weapon, while the boy scuttled behind carts and kiosks as if he had eight legs. Jacob swatted at him, but the boy disappeared down a dark alley, his large eyes shining.

Jacob then turned and declared to everyone that the boy was no longer allowed in his store if he was going to eat ice cream straight out of the container when he wasn't looking.

In the garden, a small girl in a colorful dress was fluttering from one flower to the next, taking pictures with a large camera. She would occasionally linger at one flower long enough to smell it or torch it softly, before flitting to the next.

I finished my chardonnay and turned to Anna.

"Same time tomorrow?" I asked with a grin.

"Of course!" said Anna. "I wouldn't miss the buzz for anything!"

Recognizing a Crisis When it Hits
Lemon

DIAGNOSING VULNERABILITIES
I resist the urge to pee, too nervous to leave.
My neck is sore. What happened last night?
I have not looked in the mirror today, and
there's no telling what I'll find. Although it aches, I
can't help but continue to stretch it.
Tilt, tilt, tilt! Expose, expose, expose!
Bare the skin there to be seen and wanted!
My instincts urge.
Deep down, I know what's waiting for me
in the public bathroom mirror,
next to the smudged fingerprints and soap suds.
Perhaps, that's why I'm afraid to leave despite the
desperate need
building.
I can't smell myself,
for the first time in days.

ASSESSING THE LIKELIHOOD
OF POTENTIAL CRISES
The potent combination of
chamomile, oranges, cloves,
has dispersed.
The familiar comfort
of the scent, is gone.

CRISES TYPES
It shouldn't be. It
should be right next to me.
Dammit! I had been asleep!

PARACRISES

The feeling of acid bubbles in my chest,
still warm at the thought of
what must have happened.
What do I smell like now? I can't
tell what's next, and what's not, and
the only way I'll be able to tell—
I'll have to be alone.
But there's only one place
that I can be alone: The Bathroom.
That cold, fluorescent place that
I'm avoiding.
But *god*, do I have to pee.

30 Pieces
Natalie Savage

She stood on the precipice, the bag of coins in her pocket feeling like a ball of lead. The wind was cold on her cheeks, but she could not convince herself to move.

If she had been asked a month or so ago where she thought she would be today, Arrie would have answered that she would be on her way home, warm food in her belly, and sleeping peacefully in the knowledge that her sister Karina would get the care she needed with plenty of gold to spare. She would not have said she'd be stuck standing on a frozen cliffside, watching the town below with a burning dread in her gut.

Now she regretted asking the hooded man what would befall the exiled prince she had been tasked to bring here. By all rights, she shouldn't have asked. It wasn't her business what happened after her mark had been delivered into the lion's den. But she'd always been a curious person, and the prince had a reputation for being a brave and fierce warrior. He would not be an easy man to take down. That is, unless one flooded the town with assassins, of course.

"Walk away," her brain urged, frustrated as her boots stubbornly refused to move. "You have your money, and your sister will have her care. Walk away." It should be simple; reasonable. She would trade Prince Terran's life for her sister's and her unborn child. One life saves two. A stranger saves her family. It was an easy decision, she had thought.

But that was before the caress of his fingers was branded into her skin so much so that, even now, she could still feel his warmth. That was before the twinkle in his stormy eyes caused her stomach to flip inside-out. That was before she'd tasted his lips and felt his body over hers.

A snowflake dripped down her cheek, then another, and, when she wiped her face with a frown, she realized she was crying. Her feet finally moved but, in rebellion to every instinct in her body save her heart, she was heading back to the inn where she'd left him oblivious to the fact that he would be dead by dawn.

She all but tore the door to the inn down in her panic. Despite her relatively good state when it came to physical fitness, she gasped for breath, her eyes effortlessly meeting Terran's despite not knowing exactly where in the room he would be. He looked startled and confused, a tankard of ale held halfway to his lips. The heat in the room was like entering an oven.

"We have to go," she blurted out, Terran immediately reaching for his sword.

"What's happened?" he asked, rising to his feet and dropping a few coins on the table for the innkeeper, who was, at this point, glaring at Arrie.

"I'll tell you when there are five hundred miles between us and this town," she said, reaching for his hand and pulling him towards the door. His grip in hers was strong and steady, and she was grateful for it when she noticed the dirty looks everyone in the room was giving her. "Maybe six hundred."

The door slammed in her face, a burly, tattooed arm still blocking it. Silver flashed at his hip and Arrie cursed her stupidity. Terran's grip tightened in hers as every assassin in the room stood up.

"We were going to kill him in his sleep after an evening of warm food and rich ale," the man at the door said, reaching for his dagger. "Now, we won't be as kind."

The room descended to chaos. Terran's sword cut through the air, and the man was only just able to block it. Cursing her lack of a weapon, Arrie grabbed the nearest chair and broke it over the head of the next closest man, taking his sword when it clattered to the ground. While her movements weren't as fluid and practiced as Terran's, she was hardly a slouch with a blade, and the next several men found that out quickly when they set upon her, seemingly having conflated her small stature to mean an easy target.

Still, it mattered little for they were hopelessly outnumbered. "Arrie, can you reach the door?" Terran shouted, grunting as he blocked another downswing. She glanced to it and saw at least five men between her and the door.

"No!" she shouted back, ducking as a blade sliced through the air a few inches above her head. Then she smirked at the sight of a relatively large window about five paces away. The man attacking her lunged again and she dodged to the side, using the force of his momentum to guide him through the glass.

"Terran!" she yelled, jumping through it. He followed, wincing at the slice of a blade on his forearm, but ultimately leaping out the window with relative ease. They sprinted to the edge of the town, making for the tree line. They hid in the shrubbery until the men passed them by, then cautiously splintered off into another direction, trekking to the forest. About a half a mile later, Arrie found a small cave.

"This should be safe enough for now," she said, searching to the back and nodding in satisfaction when she found it completely empty. "Tonight will be cold, and we'll need something to block the wind since we can't light a fire."

Immediately, she was pinned against the stone wall, gasping as his mouth crashed against hers. She relaxed into the kiss, burying her hands in his hair. He froze and, in the haze of his kisses, it took her way too long to realize why.

The hand on her hip moved into her pocket, pulling out the bag of gold she had long since forgotten about. He released her as if she burned him, the bag falling to the ground, coins clanging on the floor.

"I had hoped you simply overheard something as you were leaving," he rasped finally, not meeting her eye. "Tell me this isn't what it appears to be."

Arrie slumped against the wall. "My sister's pregnancy wasn't going well, and I needed money to get her care. Otherwise, I'd lose them both."

"And so you thought to trade my life for theirs." It wasn't a question, and his voice lacked any affection that it once had.

"I was wrong," she whispered, glancing up at him before looking down again, wilting from his glare. He was silent for a moment, and then turned away.

"So was I." He sat against the wall opposite her, staring to the cave entrance as if the snowfall would distract him from the tears he couldn't fully hide. She didn't bother trying.

Ants
Tyler Shea

As I look down
at this colony of ants
moving in uniform lines,

I wonder what drives them
to accomplish tasks in such
a robotic manner,

it almost makes me sad
to see such creatures
move about with no recognition of one another.

Oh, I guess the ride is over.

Title: Unknown
Arial DeGroff

Did you care at all, if ever?
Our glass castle fractured long ago,
yet you never failed to leave fragmenting
foundations built upon inconsistencies.

Pouting lips, tear filled eyes,
and peppermint freckled cheeks
never aged away from the baby fat
desperately clinging to prove
that meals resided in your stomach.

How does it feel to be best friends
with an empty Mike, no longer hard
as you sucked his insides dry?
We both did, but you've always
made more time for him.

Long ago, we were titled princes,
conquering each purple polka dotted
dragon that dared spray acid
green flames upon our land.
The remaining fog glows,
unwilling to move on,
still needing more to say.

That title walked out years ago,
suffocating brother in the process.
And I know you don't care,
would never be caught asking,
        but I'm okay.
                Besides, being
                        unknown suited me
                                better anyway.

Ideasthesia
Vinny Cucuzza

He could feel them on his skin. His feelings. Or the feeling something, someone, somewhere, gave him. Like the parts of his brain that felt emotions were linked to his skin.

There were shows that would do it. The shows that seemed disorganized and run-down felt like sludge on his arms, something to wade through. The places that he didn't want to be felt sticky. Like his skin was coated in something he couldn't wash off.

His sister made him feel like pressure built under his skin and left him feeling his arms and legs go restless because static filled them.

There were places he would think of that made him feel wrong on his skin. Italy, his family's home, made his skin feel tight, like there were things pulling on it from the inside.

The sludge on the side of the street and coating the ground felt slimy, caught on his skin.

Somewhere along the line he'd heard of synthesia. The blending of senses. A sight brought from sound, a taste from as visual, a sound from a taste.

There was a branch on the topic, in a sub-grouping on a website. Ideasthesia, they called it. A melding of thoughts or emotions and the senses. Something he was fairly aware of.

It was cool at times. His decisions were easy to make. If it felt wrong on his skin then he wouldn't do it. Easy decision.

If something didn't feel like anything it was usually fine in his mind. A kind of no warning bell, the canary keeps singing, the walls in the mine stay strong.

Although, well, it was cool until it wasn't.

And it wasn't all of a sudden.

If-is image the right word?—got caught in his head, sticking to his consciousness. And then he felt it, not the actual image, but the stuck thoughts.

A broken finger, a tear in his flesh, something that isn't him inside his body. a strong sensation of *everything* burst down his arm and into his fingers, his hands, his whole body.

Not broken.

In his head like a mantra.

Not broken.

"We're so damn slow." Lexi leaned back onto a table set against and bolted to the wall. She was holding a set of metal grippers and a long, plastic spatula in the other. "Wanna trade out times?"

"I'm here until nine-thirty, you close. Hell no."

Luciano jumped onto the table next to Lexi. The table felt warm under his thighs. "As much as I need the hours I want to go home."

The ovens filled the air with static, hot, dry air. They were loud, too. Really loud. He hadn't noticed at first but at the end of a shift he's talking louder than he should. The cold coming through the open drive-through window balanced it out a bit. If you stood too close it was a bit freezing. Give and take, Luciano guessed.

"You got a pizza coming out," Luciano hopped off the table, grabbing a pizza cutter in the same sweeping motion. "If there's a second one, we're racing."

"No, we're not," Lexi grabbed the one half out of the oven. "You just want to flex your ego. I'd win anyhow."

"You lost last time."

"Did I? I can't remember. I think I won."

"I remember differently."

"I think I won, you're the loser here. Watch your hands, dipshit."

"Love you too." He lifted his hands from the box. "That is way too saucy."

"Yeah, that has way too much on it. It's heavy as hell, too." Lexi hoisted the round pan into the air, lifting the pizza from the metal. She pulled the pan from under the pizza and dropped it onto the box, splashing some sauce onto the flat stack of boxes.

"You gonna cut it or are you gonna give me the cutter?"

"I'm doing it, quit'cher bitchin'."

Luciano cut it down the center vertically, then horizontally, diagonally on either side. "It's off center."

"Lexi, you're off center."

"Fight me."

"Gladly."

"Is there a second one?"

"It's empty, dude, we've sold one pizza in the last twenty-five minutes. You woulda called it back if there was a second one."

"You could have," Luciano flipped her off.

She ignored his finger. "You're the one in the hoodie, I'm not going—and haven't gone—anywhere near that window."

"Whatever. You're wearing pants and I'm in shorts." Luciano thrusted his hands towards the box. On the way down the tip of his finger caught on the edge of the stack, bending it back. "Ow, fuck."

A thought, one that shouldn't have lasted more than a second, caught in the web of his mind, woven by his brain.

Broken.

'Nope,' Luciano thought. 'Please no.'

He flexed his hand, splaying his fingers and curling them in. 'Not broken. I can move them.'

'I can move them.

'I can move—

'I ca—'

Broken.

Split down the center, tip too far tilted for it to be straight. Twisted, broken, pull up on the bone.

"You alright?" Lext leaned back against the table.

"Looked like it hurt a bit."

"It's fine," Luciano said. His hand spasmed, clenching and unclenching in a matter of seconds. The muscles in his arms tensed somewhat, a coil twisted until near shatter.

"Alrighty then." She stood there, staring at Luciano. "You gonna sticker that?"

His hand kept clenching. Why? His hand was fine. Not broken. *Not broken.* He flexed it again; the bones felt right, all in place. Not broken along the middle. It felt like it thought.

The image seared across his mind's eye, and he flinched. "What? Oh, yeah. Sure."

He grabbed the box and spun it around, front end facing the front of the store. 'They work, see. They work just fine. I couldn't spin this without all of them, especially without them hurting.'

Broken. Check again, you don't know. They feel it, don't they?

'They feel something, not feel pain.'

You don't know what a broken anything feels like, it could be broken. Check again.

He clenched his fingers. No pain. The sensation dropped too. A whisper, involuntary, mirroring the

74

hopes that speaking will bring it into being, "See, nothing broken."

The back of the warmer opened with a pull. Luciano slid the box onto the shelving inside. His hand twitched, fingers tightening. 'Not broken.'

Broken.

'Not broken!'

Broken, check again.

'Fuck.' Luciano flexed his hand again, the feeling and thoughts faded. For a second at least.

The drive-through window dinged. Lexi sat on a stack of boxes, leaning back against the wall. "Your turn, Luci, I just got comfortable."

"Whatever, asshat." He forced nervous, ragged breath into something adjacent to normal breath. He gripped the cold metal of the window's handle and slid it open.

Luciano's attention split itself—something he wished it didn't do on its own—between his not broken-*broken* fingers and the customer's order. Bread and a pizza or something, a pickup from forty-five minutes ago. The total was close to ten dollars.

They drove off without returning Luciano's "Have a nice night!"

Another car came through. Similar order, Luciano couldn't turn off his brain. His hands kept twitching on their own. He'd lost control of every involuntary motion of his hands; his unused hand, hidden under the drive through's blocked underside, moved incessantly, which was driving Luciano absolutely insane.

Every time he blinked, he saw a breaking finger, the bone split down the middle. Every time he saw that his hands would clench into fists and he would twist his face into a grimace.

Soon enough cars wrapped around the building. Lexi was up, moving at her max speed. After every complete cut she threw her cutter to the side, flipping the sides and securing the folds in the boxes. She and him were neck and neck with most things, cutting and boxing one of them. He was better at spontaneous racing; he didn't get performance anxiety.

This type of anxiety, though, he was all too familiar with.

Eventually the rush stopped. Cars stopped coming, the bell stopped dinging, and the ovens stopped unloading an annoying amount of food.

His brain hadn't stopped. For some reason he couldn't shake the thoughts.

Luciano kept side eying Lexi. 'Maybe if she told me they weren't broken I'd be able to calm down.'

He argued with himself for what could have been an eternity in his head, but in all actuality was eleven minutes.

"Fuck it," he pushed himself from the drive through wall. "Lexi, I need you to not judge me here."

"I can't promise that."

"I need you to, okay? Being completely genuine here."

She squinted at him, concern falling onto her face.

"Uh, yeah, sure. What's up?"

Luciano raised his hands. "Are my fingers broken?"

"What?"

"Just tell me they aren't, please. That would be very helpful." The bell at the window went off again.

"Yeah, no, they're not broken. Look fine."

Relief flooded his head. "Thank fuck. You're amazing, thank you."

His brain stayed quiet for a few minutes, enough to give him a reprieve, before starting again. It wasn't as bad though.

Progress.

Not broken.

To Find Freedom
A Free Puppet

Falling
Down
Feels
So
Freeing.

I can't say I know where I'll land.
Everything feels as though it's getting warmer.
The wind is whipping through my hair.
I can't say for sure how long I've been falling

But I can't say that I care. I am free here.

This insistent heat has burned away my wings.
Perhaps it's boiling my blood as well.
And still I cannot see the ground.
I can't say for sure if I'll still live by the time I can.

But I can't say that I care. I am free here.

Unstifled
Unburdened
My mind in anarchy
Only captive to gravity.
I've never felt so free.

side B

A Live Autopsy
Emily Price

The warmth of the skylight seeped into my skin. I felt my mother's hand press into my shoulder. It was different than the dry, cold palms that I remembered. I briefly fought the desire to shake it away, but I let it stay. Her voice dripped like the honey off a tree.

"Stell, sweetie, get up off the floor. You're going to hurt your knees."

I hated that.

I hated the way she always pushed her own insecurities on me. She was the one turning fifty-seven next month. Not me.

Yet, I begrudgingly stood up. Even as an adult, obedience always seemed to win over when I was with my mother.

"Leanna," my father said, a warning tone.

"It's ok, Clive. We just need to get her up and moving."

She clasped her long, lacquered fingers under my arm pit and hoisted me up. I felt my weight hang on her as I stood up wobblily.

It had been a long night.

Of waiting?

Of expectation?

I knew it was going to happen, and I was sorry to say that I wished it happened quicker. I wish there was less pain before the birth of his death.

My heart was wrung out in my chest and my stomach felt nauseated with an emptiness beyond hunger.

"Have you called off work, *honey*? Stell?"

What was all this *honey*? Where was any of that before he died? It was as if she was trying to call out the little girl she knew, but the little girl would not answer.

I wasn't *little* anymore.

"Leanna." There was that tenseness in his tone again. "Be gentle with her."

"I am, I am. I just don't want her to lose her job on top of everything else. I'll call them myself if I have to."

"I've got it," I said. My voice was raspy and hardly above a whisper, "I'll call them. Where's my phone?"

"Um, I think it's on the table," she said.

I grabbed my flip-phone and dialed. My hands shook as I pressed the call button.

He would have laughed at my struggle. The way I could talk to people for hours yet couldn't make a short phone call. What I would have given to hear it one more time . . .

"Hello? How can I help you?"

"This is um . . . Stella Orpheus. I can't come in today."

"Stella who? Did you have a shift in the Quilliam F. Art Gallery today?"

"Yes. Nine-forty to three-fifty."

"Alright. You are calling off for the entire shift?"

"Yes."

"I'll make note of it. Is Nadine your manager?"

"Yes."

"Ok. Bye now."

"Bye."

I set my phone back down on the table. It was the first time I could bring myself to look beyond it at the empty hospital bed. The layers of sheets were askew and there was a slight indent from where a body once laid.

I wish I felt more than an ache inside.

I wish my eyes weren't so dry.

Loss felt like an autopsy on someone who was still alive.

All for Show
Isaac Brady

The producers only showed up when something threatened their precious profits. That's when we knew that this was something major. When we got a call from the producers to attend a meeting, we knew something was up. We assumed that it had something to do with Mr. Diamond; more demands about his image, no doubt.

"Look! He's on a childrens' show, the man must be nice. Well, at least nicer than that mean ol' Malick. There's no way we're going to vote for him."

I'd heard that the network was in some dire financial straits, and if we got this guy into office, then maybe he'll just so happen to decide to send some funds our way. Or should I say, the producers' way.

The meeting was held inside our costume warehouse, which signaled to us that this was a meeting of desperation. I was sat with Mr. Nance (we both served as production assistants) next to where we kept the rabbit costumes. Mr. Sacks strolled in at about 2:35 and asked for something to stand on. Someone gave him a rickety office chair. He started with . . .

"Hello everyone. I don't know if you know me, but I'm one of the producers, Tom Sacks."

There were a few scattered, half-hearted greetings to this random guy. We didn't question who he was because none of us kept up with who was who.

"I have some news regarding Dippy the Clown, he's been arrested. Details are sparse. He sounded like he had too much juice, if ya' know what I mean . . ."

He held a fake cup to his lips and drank. This motion conjured a fake guffaw from one of the interning suck-ups; this was clearly the wrong move as Mr. Sacks only glared at him before going on.

"As you all know, Mr. Diamond is a very important client, and so, we need someone to fill in for Dippy. I'll be handling the props. But we obviously need someone to act as Dippy. And since he won't be getting paid this week, whoever volunteers will get his paycheck."

We all raised our hands. Dippy (real name: Seth) is one of the most well-paid performers on TV right now. He never discussed his pay with us normal people, but we all heard a thing or two through the grapevine. Mr. Sacks first disregarded the interns, then the women, the older men, and those he considered to be too fat or too tall (which didn't make sense as Mr. Sacks seemed both fatter and taller than Seth). When there were about twenty of us left, he randomly picked someone; that's why I was on stage that day.

Mr. Diamond had been forced to wait for an intolerable five minutes, and so I was rushed into costume and makeup. It took about seven minutes for me to get all of it on. I thought that there was no reason why Seth should be getting as much money as he gets, shit's easy.

I greeted Mr. Diamond ten minutes before we began filming. The day before, he and Dippy (he refused to call him by his real name) had practiced the routine so he was all ready to go. The routine was the same for every guest. Read two "random" letters from fans (a.k.a. the producers or their children) and then perform what they asked. The third letter always ends with a pie in the face.

"What humility! Just what I want from an elected official . . ." It wasn't long until the curtain rose onto an empty studio. Despite his practice Mr. Diamond insisted that there be no live audience for the taping. I guess he was worried about cursing in front of grade schoolers. We made our way to the letter sack and began.

"Well kids, it's almost the end of the show, you know what that means . . ."

I put my hand to my ear to receive the kids' reply (this would be added in post-production). "That's right, we're going to be opening some letters from you boys and girls at home. Mr. Diamond, would you like to open the first letter?"

"Absolutely Dippy. Let's see, this first letter comes to us from Cassandra S. from Nome, Alaska. She says she wants to watch us ride around on tricycles. Well Cassie, this one's for you!"

I wasn't incredibly skilled at riding such a tiny tricycle (do they make adult tricycles?) but neither was Seth, so I think I did well. The instant Mr. Diamond got on, he just about bust his ass. I don't think he actually practiced at all. It took him ten minutes to even start balancing on the thing. In the end, we told him that we'd get a body double and just add his face on.

"Well, Dippy, that was real fun. I wonder what this next letter says. It comes from Alice S. from here in Houston, Texas. It reads, 'Mr. Diamond I hear that you have a balanced and efficient plan for dealing with immigration while also not raising taxes on the middle-class, could you pwease explain it to us children at home?'"

The camera zoomed in on Mr. Diamond's face and he gave an impassioned explanation of his scheme to the children at home. Mr. Sacks brought out a ballot box for the final segment. After finishing his pseudo-rant, Diamond pulled out the final letter. He struggled to get it open and just ended up ripping it in an ugly, unprofessional manner. On the second take, the envelope was pre-opened and presented to him by some long-suffering assistant. Disregarding the child's name, Mr. Diamond decided to skip to the most important part.

"'Hey Dippy. Hey Mr. Diamond! I would really like you to engage in the democratic process of voting!' Well, Dippy, doesn't this sound like a wonderful idea!? Grab those ballots."

I handed him a ballot and pretended to carefully consider my choices. Walking over to the box, we dropped our votes in and put our hands to our ears so that we could pretend to hear a splat (also to be added in post). Faking confusion, I went to open the box. It wouldn't come apart. Diamond gave me shit, like he didn't just have trouble on the trike.

All at once, a bright green fog or mist or gas began to shoot from the slot where we'd placed our votes. Mr. Diamond must've thought it was part of the pie reveal because he took a deep whiff of it. I tried to look for Mr. Sacks, but he had already scurried away. That's all I know of him.

As Mr. Diamond collapsed, I pulled my party hat over my nose and mouth and headed towards the main exit. A production assistant beat me there and jiggled the handle. Locked. A stampede formed as we ran towards the exits backstage. Tables, chairs, props, and people were ruined as we pushed them out of our way. The back door was unlocked and we ran into the afternoon sun. Looking behind me, I saw nothing but a hot pink cloud. As the fog tried to seep into the fresh air, someone slammed the door shut. We could hear some unfortunate souls inside crying out in pain. At one point, I think someone on the other side tried to open the door. I don't have much more to say. I was really only worried about myself, to be honest.

I swear that the above statement is all I know about the incident in question.

Signed,
Simon Brown

Laura
Scott Kenimond

yesterday was frigid.
algid winter winds
cut through my soul
just like the news of
her sudden death

it was 9:42 when I learned
she had passed in silent slumber
as I slept peacefully
in the warmth and grip
of his snug embrace

safe from worry
safe from harm

in the few short hours
that exist between
dusk to dawn
she became just another
fucking number

not a person
not a mother
not a friend
not a woman

just some more
media propaganda
stupid statistics
scaring society
shitless.

what is the truth
what is the lie
who will live
who will die
no one really knows

the only truth right now
is that yesterday I lost a friend
as I slept comfortably
against his chest
Omicron stole her last breath

Home
Jacob Fairfield

Stepping out the door of a rustic, country-style farmhouse, I feel the subtle warmth of the bright glow of the sun setting over hills of tall grass. A lone, abandoned tractor rests, frozen in time. The field stretches for miles it seems, and I can hear the leaves of a tree beside the house rustling in the wind. Walking out onto the wraparound porch, I inhale the fresh countryside air and close my eyes, taking a brief pause to gather my thoughts and appreciate my surroundings. A couple seconds pass, and my eyes open once again.

I wander over towards an old barn sitting a short distance from the house. The gray wood paneling is illuminated with a bright orange glow. Slowly, the door creaks open, and out comes a dozen sheep pouring into the fenced off field. Exiting the fenced off area, I hear the door from the farmhouse open. Out comes a child, no more than five years old, holding in her hands a worn stuffed bear. I smile and wave at her, and she begins running towards me, her head barely peeking over the grass.

The little girl outstretches her arms and jumps into mine as I hoist her up. Strolling around the fence, we both point at the sheep as they roam across the field. A bright smile appears on the girl's face as we make our way towards the lone tractor. I sit down with her on my lap, and pull her in closer, kissing the top of her head. The girl, clutching her teddy bear, relaxes and begins closing her eyes. I turn my head towards the sunset, once again pausing to listen to the grass and the leaves blowing in the wind, and to feel the warmth of the sun on my skin. Time passes, and the light begins to fade, yet there I remain, still gazing into the night sky.

Ghost or Guardian Angel
Anonymous

When I was in high school, my father decided that he wanted my siblings and I to have a family dinner. I remember being less than thrilled, as "family dinners" have never really been my thing. Conversation mixed with the scrape of silverware against plates fills the restaurant. As we're waiting for our entrées, my father pulls from his pocket something that is wrapped in tissue paper and hands it to me. When I unfold the paper, I see a gold crucifix pendant with its chain missing. I look up and notice everyone at the table is staring at me as I turn the pendant over in my hands. "It belonged to my best friend," he said. I side-eyed my older siblings wondering if they'd heard this story before. They had.

Over dinner, my father told me the story about his best friend Martin, who had been a great influence in my brother and sisters' lives. Not long after I was born Martin fell ill and died. A few days before he passed away, he took off his three crucifix necklaces and told my father to give one to each of us. I was still looking at the necklace as my father told the story. My brother commented, "If you ever needed a guardian angel, it would be him." When I got home that evening, I put the pendant in a small jewelry box and didn't think about it again for a long time.

The next time I thought about the necklace was when I woke up and saw a man standing in the corner of my room. To be exact, it wasn't actually a man. It was more of a shadowy figure that was tall with broad shoulders. Once I blinked the figure was gone. I was thinking about that ghostly figure on my way home the next day. It had been snowing, and the road was covered in a thin layer of ice. There was a semi on the shoulder of the highway, and as I moved into the other lane my car began to fishtail. I was a hair's breadth from colliding with the car in the next lane. By some miracle, my car righted itself and I was able to exit the highway unscathed. It almost felt as though there was an actual force between my car and the one in the next lane. As I drove the rest of the way home, I remembered my brothers' words about Martin, and I thought about the figure I saw in my room. At that moment, I had never been more grateful to have someone watching over me.

Is It Raining There?
Lemon

Dear [Redacted],

They remind me a lot of you. Even in photos, I find myself second guessing despite their appearance and all of the little things I notice they do when they think nobody is watching. Things that I've trained myself for, but have yet to accomplish. They are nothing like you. Against your seriousness, your soothing moon, they are a guilty goofy sun. Will I be like them one day too?

An empty chair, where another one who is nothing like you usually sits; sugary sweet like cotton candy on an amusement park night is— what I once expected. Instead, I received burnt sugar compliments in the forms of insults and punches that I more than willingly accept. They too, are nothing like you.

This one, probably unsurprising to you, is also not like you in the slightest. I wonder what fills their head at night. The dreams that result in sad sounds is all I can hear. And still, I find myself taking more. And when I attempt to pay my debts in apologies, I'm rejected, leaving with more in my pockets. In fact, no one else is like you.

They're quiet and distant like a blurry picture of a swing set at night. It's to the point I don't know exactly what, or how, to write. They could be more like you than I know, in the way I want to ask, how are you today?

Love Always,
[Redacted]

The Woman
Isaac Brady

"There's nobody here. She's performing for nobody."
- T.

[Women can't be seen.
    They're forced to wade through darkness
        as they paddle their cars back home.
A woman is a woman.
    I should know, I have a friend.
        Her Vans glow in the dark.
There are no women here.
    {Some sexist bullshit}
        Would they be allowed what they need?
I'm here.
    With a gift from my father.
        They say I shouldn't be able to have it.]

As the form recedes,
my daughter watches
it return to the submarine land
of her fantasy.

Vacation
Jacob Fairfield

Lena always hated driving. There was just something about it that didn't appeal to her. Being cooped up in a metal box as you drifted down the highway at seventy miles per hour wasn't something to get excited about in her mind. But there was one trip every year that made her question that mindset. Every spring break, she and a couple of friends would get together and drive down to the Outer Banks. However, surprisingly to Lena, what she enjoyed most about this trip wasn't the destination, not that there was anything wrong with it, but rather the thirteen-hour road trip that brought them there.

There was something special about waking up at three in the morning to head over to her friend's house in preparation for the big trip. They gathered their suitcases full of clothes packed the night before and other necessities one would need on vacation, and tossed all of it in the trunk of her friend's Dodge Journey. This would be their home for the day, and it wasn't a problem at all. As soon as all the luggage was packed nicely into the back of the car, Lena and her three friends each chose their preferred seat before departing.

Being able to listen to music and watch movies with her friends in the backseat is what made the trip so special. They would pass cute little towns and eat at local restaurants on the way there. It was all about enjoying every aspect of the journey. Once they reached North Carolina, seeing the ocean never failed to put a smile on Lena's face. Eventually they would reach their destination, and while most of her friends only now began to appreciate the fact that they were on vacation, for Lena, it began as soon as they left home.

Backyard
Jacob Fairfield

I remember waking up in the morning for school just waiting for 2:30 to roll around. The school day itself was by no means unbearable, but what came after was far better in comparison. The bell would ring, and we would all rush to our lockers to grab our belongings before heading out the doors. Being so close to the school, all I had to do was cross the street to reach my house. After making the short journey, I would toss away my bookbag into my room before changing into some clothes more suitable for the outdoors. From there, my brother and I would hop on our bikes and head down a few blocks to our friend's house.

Jack's house was old—very old. Because of this, we rarely ever hung out indoors, and instead opted to hang out in the backyard. Each day was like a new adventure, and what we did was entirely improvised and unplanned. One day we'd play football before heading down to Dairy Queen after we became bored, and another day his younger sister would join us, and we'd all sit and talk on the playset. Eventually, when the backyard became too limiting, we would ride our bikes around the neighborhood, peddling up and down the blocks. Everything seemed so simple, and with each new day came a new memory.

Sometimes, my friends and I do miss this period in our lives. There was nothing to worry about (nothing serious anyway). I miss that old black and blue bike that had no breaks due to the amount of use it saw throughout the years. I miss drifting into the driveway and dropping the bike straight onto the gravel. Eventually though, these days began to drift away, although we always kept in touch. Even though we grew up and moved our separate ways, one thing is for certain—none of us will ever forget those days, as they helped shape us into who we are now. For that, I'm grateful.

Dreams from the Southwest Wind
John Thomas

July 19,

My therapist wants me to keep a dream journal because I keep talking about all my strange dreams. Look for patterns and all that. Luckily I've got like five empty notebooks laying around I can use for that. So here's the one I just woke from.

A creature stares me down. At least, I think I'm me. It looks almost human. Or perhaps almost angelic. It has the body of a human with perfect muscles, seeming almost carved in the image of Hercules. His head though, is bizarre, it looks like that of a lion, with a mane wrapped around his neck like some sort of strange scarf. His eyes are a deep emerald color, seeming to peer into my soul. They weren't the narrow eyes of a cat though, these were distinctly human eyes, not befitting such a monstrous visage. Behind it were great wings, almost like that of an angel, but these were not the snowy white feathers an angel of the Lord would bear. They were a dark brown, speckled with white like that of a hawk or an eagle.

His right arm is extended to the side, bent up at the elbow, as if to make an oath. His left is extended the same, but with the hand pointing down, as if to direct towards Hell. Perhaps that is where he wishes to direct me. Not that he has in the many times we've met before. Through these dreams, he is one of the few constants. Perhaps he's meant to represent something.

"It's nearly time for you to make a choice, you know." The creature's voice is deep and rumbling, and echoes in my mind. It insists upon me, until I hear my voice answer back.

"You've been saying that a lot lately. What is it you want me to choose?" I asked. I had to look up to speak to him. Given my height, he's likely over seven feet tall.

"Whether or not you wake up. You could have anything your heart desires here, you know. You have me. Money. Power. All the men and women your heart desires. I cannot fathom your insistence upon returning, day after day. Can your world offer you something mine cannot?" My eyes snap open, and I awake in a cold sweat. Sometime in the night I'd cast aside my blanket onto the floor. My cat got stuck in it. I'd like to believe her screaming woke me.

July 20,

People stand in line, idly chatting while I'm seated at a table in front of them. They carry a book with my name on the cover. Did I write that? The title is the name of the book I've been writing. The man at the front of the line sets his copy down in front of me. There's a pen in my hand. I open up the book, scribbling my name in cursive beneath the title before handing it back. I'm doing a book signing? I wish I was famous enough to get a turnout like this. It feels like hours pass but the line never seems to get any shorter, it's just person after person praising my book. At least, until *he* arrives. The man with the lion head approaches the front of the line. He doesn't have the book though, his hands are in the same position they always are. Doesn't he get tired? I suppose he is just a dream. But still.

"You have quite the small imagination. You remind me of an aging Faustus. Your dreams used to be much more interesting. Perhaps I should move on." The creature's voice echoes, seeming to shake the world around it, the peoples' bodies rippling like water and the creature's voice was the stone.

"Does that make you Mephistopheles?" I inquire, trying to ignore the rippling of the world around me. It's not working, and I start to feel seasick. Is that the word for it?

"Given your reticence, you can only hope I'd be someone so . . . benign," the creature says, his head tilting as he looks down at me. "Would you like to know my name?"

"I would. If you're going to continue haunting my dreams," I said, setting down my pen, crossing my hands on the table. They started to ripple, same as the table when the creature spoke.

"I am the master of the southwest wind, harbinger of plague and the swarms of locusts. You may call me—"

His voice is cut off by a harsh screaming. I groan, reaching over to slam my hand down on the snooze button on my alarm clock. This always happens when he gives that speech. "Master of the Southwest Wind, Harbinger of Plague and the Swarms of Locusts," and never his actual name.

July 21,

I awaken in the arms of someone, holding me close to their chest, pressed up against my back. Their breathing is soft and gentle. I think they're still asleep. Not that I'm complaining, it's nice having such a warm body up against mine, wrapped together in the soft blanket. I reach back, grabbing him to hold him close.

They grumble something close to "I love you," in their sleep, tightening their hug. I groan softly, letting my eyes flutter shut to lean back into them. That's where I found him, his outline etched into my eyelids. I opened my eyes, finding him standing over my bed.

"It's time again. Make your choice. Will you awaken? Or will you stay?" he asked, though his voice is more like a command.

"I . . . five more minutes," I grumble, shutting my eyes again and trying to pull the blanket up higher, hoping to ignore the creature standing over me. Even through the blanket though, I could still see his silhouette. I tried to sleep though, cuddled with the loving stranger behind me.

"Your five minutes is up." The blanket turned to ash, and the person behind me with it. My body felt cold now as the wind whipped around my body. Am I falling? The creature stands over me, seeming to watch as I fall. It's hard to tell though, everything but the creature is fading to white. I can't find my footing though. I can't stand. I can't feel anything but the wind.

"Make your choice. You may return, or you may stay." I wake up in a cold sweat, face down on the floor, my cat laying on my back. It seems like I fell out of bed. I wish I'd been able to stay just a while longer in the dream. Even with the creature, I've not felt so . . . at peace in a long time.

Please Come Home
Arial DeGroff

The excitement bundled in the mud filled sequins bounced along with the rocks occupying my stomach. One pigtail struggled to stay, mourning the loss of her sister after the swing accident.

Not that it mattered, though.

The clock only spoke gibberish, no matter what lies Mama would spout. The sun, however, never lied about the time of day. As it kisses the abandoned wind chime of a neighbor long lost to the wailing carriage, the familiar roar of his car would announce his return. The tired door would moan out complaints of having to work as tiny legs stumble into sturdier ones. Sandpaper hands would lift the wriggling body, murmuring honey encased words quickly eaten. Warm lips would find the forehead before conversations about adult things filled the air. Not that I cared, for the steady heartbeat lulled me away from such worries.

Nothing gold can stay.

The anxiety bundled in a worn winter coat bounces with the fluoxetine that cannot settle my stomach. Strands of hair struggle to hold onto the ear, but not enough to annoy the earring after the last accident.

It doesn't matter, though.

The calendar apologetically announces the countdown as Mama tries to prepare us for the what ifs. Nothing could ever be enough as the sun climbs up the wired fence, welcoming the crusade of wailing red and blue. He would sit in the car, rooted in spot

as strange clammy hands attempt to connect pity.
His gaze only cared about the ratted seat cover,
making me wonder if he ever really cared. I knew I
should hate him, but the need to climb into his arms
and hear the forever steady heartbeat remained.

That wasn't who he was, though.

Not anymore.

Mama and a group of officially dressed strangers
would start conversations about adult things. I
needed to understand, but unsteady legs bumped
into mine. Tired stormy eyes providing salty rivers
met my muddy brown. My shaking hands lifted the
child covered in sequins, laying a freezing kiss onto
her hat. Even as the conversations of disappointing
things floated with the longing for the ghost once
there, I prayed the heartbeat was steady enough to
lull her away from such worries.

The Chick
Natalie Savage

Her heart pounded in time with the ticking of the old grandfather clock her aunt had left her. She snatched blankets from behind the sofa, knocking over the pretty, but essentially worthless knick-knacks that she'd so loved. They shattered on the hard wood floor, but Elaine didn't notice, having already moved on to the dusty lace curtains.

"Come on, come on!" She cursed under her breath as yet another dead end was reached, her fingertips smearing the lace with blood. She couldn't feel the pain. Only panic.

Elaine scanned the room, desperately searching for some inch—no, a centimeter—that she hadn't checked. But her aunt's once spotless living room had fallen into anarchy, looking as though the men in white had already ransacked it. *She said it would be here,* Elaine thought, her breaths coming in hyperventilating pants. *She said it would be here.*

She flipped the sofa, coughing as it smashed through the nearest wall and left plaster particles in the air. The clock continued ticking and toking, but her heart had long since surpassed its tempo.

A car pulled up in front of the apartment—a sleek, black Sedan. Out stepped the men in white, steps synched perfectly as they approached the door. She had run out of time.

The voice in her head screamed at her to run, to let the men have whatever they wanted and run for it. They wouldn't care about her beyond that. But no. Her aunt trusted her with whatever it was they were after, and Elaine would find it.

Then she saw it. It was little more than a blob of yellow out of the corner of her eye catching the sunlight from the torn open curtains. She sprinted over to it, clutching it to her chest with reverence she never would have expected.

In her hands lay the stupid little porcelain chick that her aunt had picked out. Elaine had always thought it the most ridiculous thing, with eyes too big for its head and a human-esque smile. She'd thought it an ugly waste of porcelain, so much so that, when her aunt left it to her in her will, she didn't bother taking it from the house. Had the men in white not followed her from the funeral, it would have been sold the next day.

Footsteps sounded up the old, creaky stairs and Elaine threw the window open and leapt onto the fire escape. The door opened as soon as she clamored down the stairs two at a time, booking it several blocks over.

When she felt she was sufficiently safe, at least for the moment, she collapsed to her knees, chest heaving. She studied the figurine, heart in her throat and praying that her guess was correct. Her hopes were beginning to plummet when she noticed a small crack where the head met the neck. Heart in her throat, she twisted the head and pulled, snapping it from the neck in a clean break. She peered inside and then replaced the head, eyes widening. A memory card.

No Savior
Jacob Fairfield

The battle raged on for hours. No one expected they could possibly keep up a siege on the castle for as long as they had, but they took us by surprise. Nightfall, along with a raging storm provided the perfect cover. Our forces were growing smaller by the minute, along with any hope that we could prevail victorious. After spending most of my time in the watchtower, I eventually ran out of arrows and was forced to retreat down into the main courtyard. The sight I arrived at was that of horror and shock. Bodies littered the ground, and a small group of allies were barricading the castle doors. By some miracle, we were able to push them back out. Although our losses were catastrophic, maybe there was a glimmer of hope after all.

This hopefulness did not last long though, as when I moved into the infirmary to check on the wounded and stock up on arrows, the main gate broke open. Whatever was left of our forces rushed to meet the enemy head on, but I couldn't join them. Fear took over, and all I could think of was escape. I snuck around the back of the infirmary, in an effort to avoid any conflict. Soldiers rushed past, paying no attention to me. As I reached the wall, I began my ascent.

The climb was not difficult, as it is something they taught us when I was young. Scaling the wall with a bit of rope was the easy part, but as soon as I reached the top, I was greeted by the wall meeting the edge of the cliff side hundreds of meters above the raging sea below. The sounds of metal clashing together began to fall silent, and I knew the battle was nearly over. As I descended further down the cliff, I eventually reached a small beach where we had kept the boats if we ever had to retreat back to the homeland. Screams filled the air, and I knew that there were people who needed me, and were counting on me. I untied the rope of one of the rafts and prayed that I could make it through the storm. I knew that the best thing I could do was to stay and fight to the end with my brothers, but unfortunately for them, I am no savior.

When I Became You
Emily Price

I only wish that the days were good or bad. I couldn't bear the fact that no adjective existed for them. They were just days.

And days.

And days.

And days.

At least they made me feel something. The thought sits and offers that tantalizing truth to me. But I also remember the *other* days.

The other days when the withdrawal symptoms hit, and it was like the horrifying drop of a roller-coaster. I couldn't stomach anything. My own mother had to hold my stringy, lank hair back to I could barf up my guts in some godforsaken Menards' toilet.

That day, we were supposed to look for supplies to renovate our apartment's kitchen. Our plans turned into time in a rushed and frantic car ride to stat care.

My life changed when I saw *you*.

My mother may have kept me alive, but *you* made life look like it was worth living. You made it look like tomorrow was worth the present pain.

I saw you every day.

Every day that my mother dragged me out to the train station, and we'd sit on that same mildewy bench, I would see your face. Every day I sat, cradling my own head in my hands from a headache or numbed by another antidepressant, you were there.

Smiling. You were smiling. I forgot that was something I used to do.

From across the platform, you made me wonder where the light came from in people's eyes. You made me wonder whether it was possible to find the light in me.

I watched you for years, appointment after appointment, session after session, and day after day until . . . you began to look like me.

It was small and steady steps that made me notice the change. We began to carry our guitar cases with us to the station. We began to have similar habits in the way we parted our hair and brushed our teeth. Slim, bony hips turned to rounded, fleshy curves.

Before the 7:45 a.m. train was required to pull in, I made the decision to meet you. From across the platform, I saw the crown of your head like always.

You were looking down and writing, writing in a journal I recognized. A tree was etched into the raw leather and the leather laces laid awry on your crossed legs.

I should say thank you, I thought.

The words play silently across my lips. I work up the courage to stand. My legs feel wobble with nerves as I walk forward. You lift your eyes, and they meet mine.

Suddenly, the train—two minutes early this time—grinds to a halt. I board speedily in hopes of seeing you.

I wrestled my luggage over the seats and pressed my face against the windows, smudged and coated with fingerprints. You're gone.

That was the day I realized I became *me* again.

Things That Make Me Say "Hmm" While Driving
Kate Tasseff

1. Those Extremely Bright Headlights. You know the ones I'm talking about. I can't think of the word—I want to say fluorescent, but that's for mid-century light fixtures, isn't it?—at any rate, they're blasting about 50% of the sun's almighty rays when really they should only use about 0.00000005%, give or take. They ride around acting like cocky fog lights when there is no fog. Blindness has increased sevenfold in all demographics above driving age and it can all be traced back to those stupid lights. You could be a philanthropic saint on par with—well, I guess even Mother Theresa got canceled, so not her, but insert the name of the best human being you've ever known—and still you're an automatic bully for owning a vehicle with those headlights.

2. Busted Signs. These come in a few different forms. The most amusing is the half-lit lettering on a building's side. There's a Hilton Garden Inn just a stone's throw from the on-ramp I take every morning, and for six months, the bold red brand name has been split down the middle, flashing in a right-side, left-side, right-side pattern at one-second intervals. I don't think "rave" is the mood that Hilton Garden wants to put out into the world, but they don't seem to be in any hurry to get it fixed.

3. Tailgaters. This is a tough one, since, if I'm honest, I've been both victim and victimizer. My defense? I'll only ride you if you're going a) *below* the speed limit b) on a one-lane road, just as a friendly reminder that you're unreasonably ruining everyone else's day. What I can't wrap my head around is drivers who tail me when I'm already cruising anywhere

from five to ten mph above regulation, *especially* when they *could* go around me but *don't*. Any helpful hint they're trying to deliver is translated into pure Jerkguage. The temptation to brake-check these folks is tempered only by the fact that my car is already on death's door and I can't afford a new one.

4. I Just Remembered the Name of Those Lights. They're LED. Of course. Carry on.

5. Corny Billboard Puns. Ohioans can back me up on this. Every holiday season, we are subjected without consent to safety messages in the form of jokes so devoid of humor that I can only assume they were written by an AI that learned everything it knows from *Gasoline Alley* comics.

Easter? They've got it covered:
DRIVE EGG-CELLENT
SOME BUNNY NEEDS YOU
Thanksgiving?
MASH POTATOES
NOT YOUR HEAD
BUCKLE UP
Christmas?
VISITING IN LAWS?
GET THERE LATE
SLOW DOWN

We need to get the boomer bots out from behind the ODOT keyboards. No puns, just vibes.

6. Traffic Jams for No Reason. There is little else in all the world that can so sap me of the will to live. I should not be forced to sit indefinitely in my car—if I wanted to do that, I'd have picked a parking lot, not this 65-mph-sanctioned asphalt ribbon of manifest destiny. A traffic jam is a perfect depiction of Christianity's original sin: "Therefore, through one man's decision to check his crypto

balance on his morning commute, all men have been condemned to suffer and die." To be fair, I can at least see the logical starting point of congestion caused by a wreck or the weather. But my mind simply melts when I arrive at the end of a twenty-minute standstill and find nothing: no accident, no debris, no Canadian protestors, no gaping sinkhole. Vanity of vanities, all is vanity!

7. My Own Road Rage. It's dawned on me that this has become a three-page rant on my pet peeves of transportation, a little less "Hmm" and a little more "@%$&!" I swear I'm not this angry in real life! But when you commute over 400 miles a week, these things tend to bottle up. I should probably steer my ire into a more meditative sort of "Hmm."

Deadly Dreams
Natalie Savage

Lyssa had been called many things in her life. Freak. Insomniac. Insane. People were kinder when she was a child, of course. Then they used phrases such as "a vivid dreamer" or "highly imaginative." No one thought it was anything out of the ordinary then. After all, why would they? Stuff like this just didn't happen in real life. If it did, she wouldn't be known as the freaky dreamer girl at school. She, personally, preferred "cursed." There was no better way to describe it.

She had been dreaming as long as she could remember, and these dreams were full of colors and lights, and creatures beyond her wildest imagination. She'd seen purple oceans and forests made out of glass. She'd seen candy houses, floating castles, and skies with more moons than she could count, each glowing like the bioluminescent algae she'd studied in science class. She'd made friends with fairies, swam with finned tigers, flown on griffins, and raced a bear with the head of a guinea pig across a frozen tundra of sugary snow.

She had been filled with such wonder and amazement that she had seen this as a gift; an opportunity to escape her ordinary life filled with school and homework and go on her own adventures in lands closer resembling the fairy tales her mother had told her. Every night was different and, every night, she would go to sleep in eager anticipation of what the coming night would bring.

But then, as she grew older, her dreams grew darker. At first, they weren't much different than nightmares anyone else would have, so her parents didn't think much of it. Being chased by an army of flying skeletal sharks was just a scarier version of the glowing flying eels she had seen the week before.

But her parents finally believed her when the finned tiger was replaced by mermaids who, while at first looked friendly, ended up dragging her kicking and screaming to the bottom of the sea to devour her. She had woken up spewing sea water and screaming, her skin covered in scratch marks from their nails.

The oceans were replaced by boiling water that burnt her skin. The glass forests were replaced by literal blades of grass that cut her feet. The candy houses caused sores in her mouth. The floating castles were haunted by screeching dragons with the body of snakes. Asteroids fell from the moons and released translucent worms that burrowed under her skin.

Her stories had told her that curses were put on innocent princesses by evil witches out of hatred and spite. Apparently, however, her evil witch must have hated her even before she was born.

Since then, she couldn't sleep, prominent bags appearing under her eyes no matter how much she tried to hide them under make up. Her life was a one-way ticket to misery and torment. She couldn't focus in school with no sleep and she couldn't sleep without being tortured by creatures and worlds that shouldn't be real but somehow were.

Her extended family knew her as insane. Her doctors, an insomniac. Her classmates, a freak.

All she knew is that she wanted sleep. A boring, dreamless sleep.

Memento Mori
Tyler Shea

A true image of the macabre
Glares at me from the canvas,
Injecting a feeling of darkness into my veins.

The back pits of the skull
Remain familiar and inviting,
Yet horrifying and dark.

It is an image that reminds me of death,
not in a horrific way,
but as a reminder that it will always catch up.

High Feelings at Sunset
Lexus Thornton

Memories of you come flooding back to me,
as I witness the ball of fire setting above the horizon

You were as bright as the sun, who would give life
    to us.
Like that bright star, you gave life to me.

Yet, like the sun, you had to quietly disappear from
    my life.
And in came the moon that would be temporary as
    you.

But, unlike you I could still see this moon when you
    are out.
The moon seems to illuminate me more in my dark-
est hours.

I will still miss your sun kisses and warmth, but the
    moon will give me her moonlight and safety.

The Wild West
Jacob Fairfield

When I was a freshman, there was nothing I wanted more than for my morning classes to end, and for lunch to begin. Every day, following the same routine. As soon as that bell rang, I quickly rushed to my locker to grab the same brown paper bag I always brought, and met up with my friends as we marched down the hallway towards the cafeteria. We turn into the large room, spotting our signature table, the second farthest from the entrance, closest to the stage with the giant projector screen which our weekly announcements would play from every Friday. Each of us shared stories of what happened throughout the day, laughing, joking, simply having a good time. Eventually, the same bell would ring, signaling the end of this joyous occasion in the day and beginning the wait until tomorrow.

Come senior year, the safe space that was the cafeteria at lunchtime quickly changed into what could only be described as the wild west. As my friends and I grew older, so did our insecurities and our views on school itself. Our table, second farthest from the entrance, became some other freshman group's safe spot. As for my friend group, we now had been eating lunch in the farthest room in the building, where we had gotten permission from our teacher to use in order to avoid the cafeteria. Gone were the days of mindless fun, laughing without a care in the world as if we were in our own little bubble. Where there used to be around twenty, became a mere four individuals watching television shows and eating our lunches away from the rest of civilization.

Although distant, we did not completely ignore this vast wasteland where people formed tight knit communities that watched and judged each other. Every Friday, we ventured in to play the weekly announcements, watching from a distance and trying to piece together where everything changed; when we broke out of our little bubbles and began to become overwhelmed by everything around us. After finishing, we would rush back to our safe room, waiting out the time until the bell rang, beginning again our new cycle of waiting. Once, the wait was unbearably long, and could not come soon enough. Now, walking back to that distant room in the back of the school, we all catch glimpses of the wild west of a cafeteria, wondering what we ever saw in it.

Road Trip
Jacob Fairfield

The car ride seemed to last an eternity. Sam knew it would be long, but this was just unbearable. The view of the desert, while breathtaking at first, became a bit dull after two days of driving. Every little bump shook the minivan so violently that she was convinced it would fall apart as they sped down the highway at seventy miles per hour. Kat had spent the last hour counting how many license plates were from California, and Evie's attention was split between driving and searching for the next cassette to play. If Sam had to sit through another Grateful Dead album, she was sure that it would be the end for her. Luckily, this wouldn't be the case, as the sun was setting once again.

The three of them pulled off the highway and drove for a bit down a beaten path through some bushes and tumbleweeds. The sun finally set, and Kat suggested they stop ahead next to a group of cars parked along the road. Exiting the car, Sam could see a group of about ten or so people gathered around a small campfire. The trio marched forward asking if they could join them. Sam thought they all seemed friendly and struck up a conversation. While chatting, they learned that the two groups had more in common than they thought. The sounds of small talk, a subtle acoustic guitar playing, and winds from the desert filled the air.

When Sam awoke, the other group had begun packing up their belongings and were almost ready to head out. Although only a brief encounter, seeing other people in the same situation as her, besides Kat and Evie of course, was surreal. The two groups said their goodbyes as the strangers headed back towards the highway. Walking back to the minivan, Sam noticed the guitar leaning against the door with a note attached, telling them to take care of it. Moments like this reminded her of why they were doing this, and why even though Kat and Evie drove her crazy, they were all in this together. As they entered the minivan and began driving again, Kat and Sam took turns playing the guitar in the back seat. The three of them continued laughing as they turned onto the highway, passing a sign that read "southern border, 150 miles out."

Decaying and Drowning
Lexus Thornton

I don't want to bloom in your arms and then wither
away with the wind taking me.

I can't prosper if the critters in my mind crawl their
way through my vessel to eat me from the
inside.

My mind is decaying as my heart is rotting.

No amount of water and fertilizer can revive me.
Too deep in this abyss to find even a ray of light.

That sun that you produced
So warm and bright.

But it was I that caused the sun to be no more.
Creating cumulonimbus clouds

Now I am causing floods to crash this physique of
mine.
Until I succumb to this water grave.

I, who was once a flower in this garden, am now
nothing but petals in this fleeting memory.

Retrograde→
Scott Kenimond

Life is a circle
planets orbit

Around the sun
fixed movement

Some circuits are quick
Others seem to crawl

At times some appear
to move backwards

←Retrograde

like feels life My
retrograde in spheres these

backwards move I As
on moving is else everyone

greatness Achieving
unravel slowly I as

me remind please Someone
illusory just is movement this

Selfish Elegy
A Selfish Puppet

Souls are souls, all shining the same.
Different from mine, dripping in shame.
Your heartfelt words mean naught to me.

Gave it all my heart
But still wasn't enough.
Carved my soul from wax
Then I touched the sun and it turned to mush.

So I'll kill that me
Who never was enough
For you.

I'll set my soul free.
I'll form this mush to wings
And fly away.

I may be dead
But at least I'm me.
This coffin six feet down
Has finally set me free.

I wrote this elegy
For me.
I don't want to hear you mourn.
I'm finally free.

I See Red
Hannah Adams

1,2,3 ...
Three red cars go by.

I wonder, why is it such a popular color? My head aches for a moment, then I'm back.

4, 5 ...

Two more pass by. I wonder, why did I choose that color to count? Because it is popular? Because it is the only color I can differentiate in my state? My vision is so blurred.

6, 7, 8, 9 ...

Four more. I wonder, can they see me? Can they see the same color on me? Another surge of pain splits through my skull, then I'm back. As back as I can be.

10, 11 ...

It's getting harder to count. They must not see me. No one heard me, so why would they see me? I wonder, did they hear, do they see, do they just not care enough?

12 ...

I can't see red anymore. I wonder, how can I count the cars if I can't see red anymore? The thought cuts through my brain. I don't feel another pain . . . I can't see red anymore . . . I can't count the cars. I see black.

It Comes Again
Hannah Adams

She sits in the sunroom of the small century-old farmhouse. She turns the page of her book, slowly bringing a small biscuit to her mouth and bites into it, feeling the crumbs slowly dissipate in her mouth and the semi-sweet taste spread across her tongue.

She suddenly looks up from the page. There is a dragging sound, like someone sliding their feet across the floor when they find it hard to walk. It comes from the attic.

The clock chimes, she looks, takes in the time, and looks back to the page. She finishes the biscuit.

The sound comes again from above.

She doesn't look up from the page. She wraps her thin pale fingers around the stem of a porcelain teacup, bringing it to her lips and letting the bitter liquid counteract the sweetness in her mouth.

The sound comes again. Louder this time. Like the walking became more labored with increasing pain.

She smiles; she turns the page, placing the cup down and grabbing another biscuit.

Her husband sure made a lot of noise for a dead man . . .

The Devil on Her Shoulder
Sean Miller

Stella had been sitting alone with a difficult decision for much of the night. It was creeping steadily closer to 3 a.m. The witching hour. An ominous and unnerving time for most, the dead of night always had quite the opposite effect on Stella. She found it to be a time of comfort and solace since her youth. Now that she was closing in on thirty and still working the same dead-end bartending job for the better half of a decade, she rarely went to bed before dawn. Thus, the witching hour was a time she often spent unwinding from long, arduous nights of serving cheap beer to the few haggard-looking individuals that frequented the tavern she worked at. But, tonight she couldn't unwind. So, she paced around her dingy inner-city studio apartment with a bottle of discount cabernet glued to her right palm.

The plan was simple. She would take the keys she received when she was appointed the position of assistant manager and sneak into the bar. Then, she would rob the safe. Her boss, Steve, had the lock combination hidden under the microwave in the break room and was too senile to remember he put it there three years back. There was only one security camera outside the front door, but the back entrance was desolate. It displayed a shady alleyway littered with dumpsters filled to the top with a never-ending supply of plastic containers and packages, discarded scraps of fast food, and all the other wasted resources deemed useless by the same capitalist overlords producing all the trash to begin with. All she had to do was take the money from the safe. Then, she would pack up the few belongings she possessed and drive her beat-up old Lincoln to wherever the hell she felt like going.

The plan was fullproof, but she just couldn't seem to justify it to herself. She didn't feel bad about robbing the owner. That wasn't it at all. Steve was the exact cliched type of ancient establishmentarian she despised. Stella could often see him watching bigoted news stations on evening cable television through the front window of his exorbitant house with the perfectly manicured yard that she just knew he complained about to his lawn care crew of underpaid minorities. No, she did not care at all about Steve and actively wished him the worst. What Stella was contemplating was deeper somehow. She felt as if simply robbing him wasn't enough. She could do more.

"Dammit," she said aloud. "If only there really were a devil on my shoulder—" A loud crashing noise rang throughout the one room apartment. Stella shrieked as she jolted her head to face the direction of the bathroom. To say the hairs on the back of her neck stood up would be an understatement. They were actively jumping off her skin.

"What the hell," muffled a disgruntled voice from the bathroom. The voice was oddly placid but clearly in pain.

Stella reached for the Louisville Slugger her father had given her for Christmas one year in a desperate attempt to get her interested in sports. "Who the hell is there?" she stammered, trying to appear unafraid.

A short, young-looking man stumbled out of the bathroom groaning. He had a messy shock of jet-black hair and was adorned in a tattered sweater with the collar of a red button-up shirt barely poking out. What appeared to be two stubby little horns jutted out of both sides of the top of his forehead. "Uhhh . . . you summoned me?" he said in a slightly annoyed manner.

"I will literally knock your head off those scrawny little shoulders if you don't get out of here right now!" Stella shouted, confidence rising.

"Dude," he said, clasping his left hand to his horns, "you called *me* here. You summoned the help of the devil. Didn't exactly mean to land on your toilet, but here I am. So what do you want?"

Stella laughed aloud. "You mean to say that *you're* the devil?"

"Hell no, I'm not the devil," he said, looking almost offended. "I mean, I am a demon. But, I am most certainly not the devil. I hate that guy. Like, he doesn't even get me, man."

"There's no way this is real," Stella thought aloud, looking at the empty bottle of wine now lying at her feet.

"Well, it certainly is real," he said, looking slightly confused. "Like, I can prove it, if you want."

"Okay, then prove it."

The young demon glared at the baseball bat in her hand, and began muttering something unintelligible under his breath.

"Yeah . . ." she said unimpressed. "Great job. I totally believe you're a demon and not some creep hanging out in my bathroom."

"Look at your hand, dummy," he laughed.

When Stella looked down at her right hand she dropped its contents immediately in horror. A brand-new bottle of discount cabernet crashed to the floor and spilled the precious red wine all over her only rug.

"Believe me now?" he questioned casually, as he took a seat on a wine-stained recliner situated directly in front of her TV. "Now, how can I be of assistance? Or whatever." He pulled out a pack of cigarettes and lit one up as if nothing out of the ordinary had just occurred.

Stella looked at the broken bottle and contemplated bolting for a second. She was still in utter shock and was honestly debating running out of her tiny apartment and starting a new life. For all she knew, this was her first hallucination in what was rapidly developing into a life-long battle with schizophrenia.

"You were deciding whether or not you should rob that bureaucratic scumbag, Steve, I believe?" he asked, not looking away from the television's black screen.

"This can't be real," Stella thought aloud, still in a catatonic state.

"Oh, it's real," the demon stated calmly. "And I gotta tell ya . . . I think it's a pretty dumb idea." He cracked open a beer that must have been another one of his conjurations, because Stella had no more alcohol in the apartment. "Like, it's such a bad idea. Just robbing them and then leaving. They would know it was you. The cops would track you down and arrest you in a couple days' time." He chuckled at the notion.

"Then what would you suggest?" she asked earnestly.

"I suggest you crack open a brew and contemplate this nonsense again in the morning."

"Why are you telling me to do the rational thing?" Stella asked. "Aren't demons supposed to encourage this sort of behavior?"

"I mean, I guess," he said, extinguishing his cigarette into his now empty can of beer. "But like ... that's kinda just a stereotype. And for a person like yourself, who hates prejudiced jerks like the owner of that dilapidated bar you work for, I really expected better."

"I am so confused right now," Stella said, as she collapsed into a seat on her couch.

"It happens. Here, have a beer." A can appeared suddenly in her palm. She opened it and quickly chugged the the tasty, yellow ale within.

"I guess, I just thought a demon would be all about promoting chaos and evil deeds," Stella prodded.

"Honestly ... I've really been getting into the idea of Buddhism lately," he pontificated. "The notion that we're like ... all one in the same ... and the idea of finding inner peace through the enlightenment of the soul really speaks to me. Like, don't get me wrong. I've done a lot of demonic stuff and all ... but, it doesn't really do anything for me. I feel like I've just been doing horrible stuff all these years because it was, like ... who I'm supposed to be? Y'know?"

Stella scoffed. "A Buddhist demon, huh? Now I really have heard it all."

"Again with the typecasting?" the demon smirked. "I really had you pegged as being a bit more ... I don't know ... socially conscious."

"I'm sorry," she quipped. "You'll have to forgive my political incorrectness, if that's what you could even call it. I'm pretty sure there aren't too many rules about stereotyping demons out there."

"It's all right. No offense taken," he stood up and threw his beer can onto the floor, a bit of cigarette ash spilling onto the carpet.

"Could you not?" Stella said, sounding annoyed.

"Conquer the angry one by not getting angry, conquer the wicked by goodness, conquer the stingy by generosity, and the liar by speaking the truth," he said, suddenly serious.

"What does that even mean?"

"Just a few wise words from the Buddha himself." The demon boy snapped his fingers and in an instant he vanished along with the beer can and two empty bottles of wine. Dumbfounded, but too exhausted to care, Stella closed her eyes and drifted off to sleep.

The next day, Stella woke up bright and early at 4:37 p.m. Not sure whether the events of the night before were real or just an alcohol-induced hallucination, she decided it was in her best interest that she not rob the bar. That geriatric bureaucrat, Steve, that employed her, deserved to have his wealth taken from him and dispersed to the lower-class people whose labor he so willingly exploited. That was for sure. But, robbing him just wasn't worth jeopardizing her own life. It wasn't her duty to teach Steve the error of his ways. She stood up and yawned before getting dressed and ready for another long night of work.

The keys twisted in the ignition to start the engine of her rusted-out jalopy, and Stella took off. The thought of going back to work didn't seem that bad. Robbing the bar wasn't going to stop capitalism. Stealing Steve's money wouldn't end a few centuries' worth of working-class oppression.

As she pulled into the decrepit alleyway behind the bar, she noticed Steve cursing loudly as he slammed the back door shut behind him. She laughed.

The tavern was dimly lit as usual. A sickly green undertone gave the room an unsettling aura. It was an atmosphere Stella had grown quite used to. Steve was fuming behind the bar.

"What's up?" she questioned calmly.

"The drawer is short fifty-four dollars," he snarled, eyes fixated on the cash register.

"You took it out of the register before you left last night. You said you had to buy a gift for your daughter. Remember?"

"I did no such thing," Steve shouted in disgust. "You stole it from the register, didn't you? You've always spited me, even though I pay your bills, girl."

For some reason, Stella thought of the night before. "Conquer the angry by not getting angry," the demon boy said as his face flashed in the recesses of her memory.

"You don't pay my bills, though," she stated with a kindly expression on her face. "The customers do."

"What did you just say to me?" he asked, frown transforming into an evil scowl.

"The state only requires you to pay me $3.50 an hour. I pay my bills with customer tips alone." She smiled and turned away.

"You ungrateful little—" As soon as Steve stepped away from the register, he fell to the ground clutching his left arm.

"Oh, my god!" Stella shrieked, running toward Steve's collapsed frame.

"You did this!" he shouted at her, writhing on the floor in the fetal position. "You knew I had a heart condition and you still decided to steal from me!"

A look of utter disdain crept across Stella's face. Everything Steve had ever falsely accused her of came rushing to the forefront of her mind. He accused her of stealing from the register every other week. On a few occasions he blamed her for low attendance rates, claiming she was locking the front door every time he left. He had once even gone so far as to profess that she was diluting the bar's liquor with anti-freeze and pesticides. Steve called it a criminal attempt to get the health department to shut down the whole bar for good. She should let him die. The world be better off without rich people that exploit others' hard work anyway.

The demon boy's face flashed in her mind's eye once again. "Conquer the wicked by goodness," his voice rang.

Stella reached for her cellphone and called the ambulance.

When the EMS arrived, they strapped Steve to a stretcher and rushed him into the back of the ambulance truck. One of the medics stayed with Stella to fill out an accident report. She filled out all the required paperwork and handed it to the EMT.

"You're probably gonna need to take over manager duties for this trash heap tonight," he laughed, before heading out into the night.

Stella glanced at the cash register, then outside to Steve's ambulance as it hauled him away. She thought about the paper with the lock combination written on it underneath the microwave in the break room.

"Well, I already took the moral high route," she thought. "Steve's safe with the medics. I saved his life. Why shouldn't I take his money and run? I do all the work anyway. It's my labor that keeps this business afloat."

The demon boy's annoying little face popped into her thoughts once again, as the words, "Conquer the stingy by generosity," echoed through the walls of her skull.

"Fine, damn it!" Stella bellowed. She sat there for the rest of the shift, serving her only three customers pitcher after pitcher of cheap yellow beer. They tipped her four dollars and stumbled out of the bar.

Sighing heavily, Stella walked out from behind the counter to lock the front door. She would be glad to go home, pop open a bottle of merlot and relax, knowing she made the right decisions today. As her hands fumbled to find the keys, she heard a loud knock at the door. A short woman with a large head stood on the other side. She looked about forty and seemed quite upset.

"Is Steve there?" the woman asked.

"Steve's not here," Stella said. "Now, if you'll excuse me, it's late and I need to get going."

"Please," the woman pleaded. "I'm his daughter."

"Uhh," Stella sighed as she opened the door. "Alright. How can I help you?"

"It's just that it was my birthday today. I was supposed to meet up with my father at our favorite Italian restaurant a few hours ago."

Stella knew where this was going.

"He never showed up, and I've been calling his cellphone for three hours straight," the woman explained. "He never misses phone calls or dinner dates, and I'm worried to death about him. Did you see him at all today?"

For a split second, Stella thought about lying and telling her he never showed up. That he probably spent day getting wasted at the casino and blowing her birthday money on slot machines. Why should she care if Steve's daughter got to see him on what could very well be his last night on Earth? That wasn't her problem. Besides, if he was anything close to as bad of a father as he was a boss, she'd be doing this woman a favor. Then, the demon boy's voice echoed though the chambers of her brain once more. "Conquer the liar by speaking the truth," it advised.

"Steve had a heart attack about three hours ago," Stella blurted out, suddenly feeling a sense of concern.

"Oh, my!" the woman gasped in horror. "What hospital did they take him to?"

"The EMT said they were taking him to Central Metro," Stella quickly responded.

"Oh, thank you so much!" The woman clasped her arms around Stella's torso in an awkward hug.

"No problem at all."

"Bless your heart!" the woman yelled, as her stubby little legs carried her off to her expensive looking SUV as fast as they could.

"I hope Steve is alright!" Stella shouted after her, the words leaving a bitter taste in her mouth.

Stella locked the door and walked to her Lincoln parked in the back alleyway. As she drove home a sense of serenity overtook her emotions.

When she opened the front door of her dump of an apartment, she headed to the cupboard. Two cheap bottles of merlot sat awaiting her arrival. She uncorked one and took a long, satisfying chug straight from the bottle.

"So, did you get that money or not?" the demon boy asked, nonchalantly. He was sitting on the recliner drinking a beer and smoking a cigarette down to the filter.

"No," she said, confused. "I took your advice."

"My advice?" he asked, genuinely bewildered. "What advice?"

"You know," Stella said, wondering if he was just messing with her. "The Buddhist proverb you quoted before disappearing last night. 'Conquer the angry one by not getting angry, conquer the wicked by goodness, conquer the stingy by generosity, and the liar by speaking the truth.' Well, I listened to all of it. And, honestly, I feel pretty good about myself. So . . . thank you. It really helped me out."

The demon boy laughed aloud. "I was hammered last night. I don't even remember saying that."

Stella sighed in annoyance.

The Sky Bleeds
Hannah Adams

Orange, pink, red, yellow
The sky bleeds

      Blue slowly disappears from the atmosphere,
            but grows quickly in your eyes

The warm light makes your chestnut hair suddenly
   seem auburn in hue

              Beautiful
          What is more beautiful?
     You? The sky? Both? Both of us, together

My skin grows warm in the sun's light
My heart grows warm in yours

          The world condemns us . . .
             but here,
        the sun, she welcomes us

The colors bring us into their warm embrace
Now, in this moment, our love is nothing but ours

         Orange, pink, red, yellow
           The sky bleeds
           and so do we . . .

The Unexplored Trauma of Black History Month
Kendra Ivery

February is my favorite month of the year. Mostly because it is Black History Month. As an adult, I've grown to appreciate the complexity of this month. For me, it has become a 28-day reflection period. I think about my ancestors, their struggles, and their achievements. I also celebrate simply being a Black woman. The Black community comes together to uplift Black voices, businesses, and history. But for me, Black History Month hasn't always been a month to look forward to. Although I've grown to embrace my Blackness and Black History Month, it was one of the biggest hidden traumas of my childhood.

During February, K-12 schools dust off their black history curriculum. For years, classes sit through lectures on slavery, Harriet Tubman, and Fredrick Douglass. Stories from the Civil Rights Movement that are meant to inspire. The non-Black children would pay enough attention to prove their "wokeness" while Black children try their best to dissolve into the background as the PowerPoint cycles through photos of slave auctions. Their non-Black classmates steal surreptitious glances when they think no one will notice. The normal topics of Black History that are discussed in the school curriculum are designed to tell only parts of the Black narrative. It pulls out all the high points of 400 years of slavery and racism. Leaving the rest of the horrifying details for Black adults to be scarred by, and non-Black adults to dismiss.

It is distressing to see features of Black women picked out of a catalog and presented to a plastic surgeon. Psychical features such as lips, chests, and butts are surgically placed upon non-Black bodies. Cultural traditions and mannerisms are caricatured by white celebrities who are so quick to put down the Black women that they try to emulate. We protest for our right to live in the streets chanting "Black Lives Matter." Only to be told to comply by those who wear bamboo earrings and speak butchered AAVE.

Black History Month has also developed a large commerciality that does not serve the community it attempts to uplift. Companies unveil lines of products that feature black people to pander to the Black community. There is a huge difference between Black-owned and Black-themed. It's embarrassing that these companies who are so quick to show off their company's diversity don't understand that difference. Acknowledging Black people during Black History Month while ignoring their struggles during the other eleven months of the year is a unique form of gaslighting that continues to harm the Black community.

An Instagram Theft
Kate Tasseff

Someone stole my Instagram photo once. She was a friend, too. Well, more like a friend-of-a-friend—or, if you really want to be precise, an ex-friend of my best friend. This is the nature of social media relations: the people you follow and who follow you often have only the loosest connection to you in the real world. Maybe you met once at a party, or studied abroad with them in college and have never seen them since, but you still get to see the pretty oak milk lattes they drink every day. It's nice.

Anyway, it wasn't so nice when this girl stole my Instagram photo. Her theft made no sense and still baffles me to this hour. By utter coincidence, we'd both been on a hike that day: it was a rare, warm Ohio Saturday in November, the kind of day to drag yourself and your significant other out of your Netflixian stupor and into the woods to see gold leaves glow against blue skies and feel alive again for precisely 58 minutes. Her hike was in Wayne County, though, mine in Summit (the Blue Hen Falls, if you must know: a stunning lack of blue hens, lame falls—gross false advertising). The foliage was at peak beauty in both our parks, so of course we both felt led to snap and share it on our Instagram Stories.

She liked my picture enough to send me a private message about it, wanting to know where I'd taken it. And so I told her, and mentioned the underwhelming falls, recommending better ones. She thanked me, and that was the end of the exchange. Or so I thought.

About an hour later, I was scrolling through Insta while my boyfriend cooked us dinner. Up popped a new post by this girl, with the caption "perfect day to go in the woods," bordered by sparkle emojis. Yes, I agree, I thought, as I swiped through the pictures of her hike with her husband, all glazed in the sorts of golden hues I'd seen myself earlier that day. But I hit the third photo and froze.

"Why does that one . . . ?"

But it couldn't be.

I tapped on my own Story bubble and looked at my picture: elongated white oaks stretching up their yellow feathered arms into *le ciel bleu* above.

I went back to her post: it was undeniably the same photo. All the rest of her pictures were hers (or were they? What was she capable of??) except that one, slipped coyly into the middle of the pack.

Flabbergasted? That doesn't begin to cover it. I started to laugh so hard that my boyfriend stepped away from his hot stove and came to see what was wrong. I showed him the evidence through a shaking phone, and he squinted and frowned and "huh!"ed several times before wandering again to the kitchen with his spatula crossed behind his back.

I put my best people on the case: my sisters + best friend group chat. I sent multiple screenshots with timestamps, and the texts fell thick and fast, punctuated by incredulous gifs and alternative theories. Could she have saved my photo for artistic inspiration and accidentally tapped it into her hiking album while selecting the others? Did she want her friends to think my (obviously superior) photo was hers, and did she think I wouldn't notice?

The investigation came to a screeching halt when, without warning, the Instagram post disappeared. I gasped, scaring my longsuffering chef boyfriend yet again. Maybe she'd realized her error (or her guilt!) and taken it down in shame. The group chat cheered. Another victory for intellectual property rights!

Only, 10 minutes later, the post was reposted.

A few photos had changed.

But guess which one hadn't?

"You know, we're living in a SOCIETY!" my best friend all-capsed.

Did I end up confronting this Instagram burglar? I did not. For a post with 28 likes (a paltry sum), it wasn't worth the fight. Whether she intended to do me harm or not, it matters little, a droplet in the social media sea. I'll let St. Peter decide whether he wants to tick this box when her time comes.

Beating Lights
Lemon

It's been a while since you've felt like this, alive.
You're panting, you can't breathe. And yet, you find
that you don't mind. You let the sparse sips of water
that your body will allow, slide down your throat,
and settle into your stomach, cool and refreshing.
It curls its way through, and the contrast is stark.
Although your insides are chilled, bone achingly so,
your skin is filled with flames.

You're panting and waiting and *hoping*. Hoping
that this time will be better, that you'll know this
song through and through. You don't. It's okay, you'll
find a way to make it work, you always do. It doesn't
matter what it looks like.

(It does.)

No one is watching.

(He is.)

All that matters is to let go. Let it out! Squeeze
every ounce of pent up power contained in the
very pads of your fingertips, in the crevices of your
nail beds, until there's not a single drop left. Surely,
something must happen this time. It's been hours
and still you have gotten nowhere near what you
need. You're still trapped, stuck in your own body,
and this is the only way you know how to be let out.
Yes this is it. This has to be the one, you think.

It's the last thought you have before you feel
that familiar lurch. If you could still think, you
might have found yourself wondering what would
happen this time; you would hope for something
flashy. You're angry, you're sad, you're lonely, but—
most of all, you're wanting.

Wanting for more than you could ever hope
to deserve, and you want it to be known. The lights
fade from red to blue to green to yellow to—your
shadow can definitely be seen from the window.
Nothing but a silhouette, dark and empty.

(You're seen.)

You're waiting and waiting and—you need
something *more!* You let your eyes drift shut, hoping
that it aids in your endeavors. You can still see the
colors pulsing, slow and gentle under your eyelids.
You open them again, to find what you've been
waiting for. It's subtle, and if you were anyone else
you would have missed it because you know anyone
else wouldn't believe you.

(He would.)

You closed your eyes again, partially satisfied, and
suddenly you can feel his breath trickle against the
sensitive flesh of your skin. You sigh, allowing your
breath to mingle and merge with his. You lift your
arm up, and he pushes you playfully to make you lose
balance. You do, and try not to giggle in amusement
as you correct your falling form, starting the small
movement again with a soft smile. He lets you go
through with it this time, standing back just to watch.

You lift your other arm up to match the first,
and his hands grip hard, digging into your swollen
hips. You roll your head, and it exposes your neck,
to which he blows a breath. You shiver and expose
the other side because symmetry is crucial, and he
pushes you again, harder this time. He doesn't like
to be ignored. You fall into the armchair behind you,
but you refuse to falter. You stand, eyes blazing.

A trail of determination and desperation fol-
lows you as you begin again. Right arm up, left arm

up, head to the right, head to the left, then forward and up. The gaze he carries is heavy against your form. You should feel sick, but you don't. *You keep going.* Your skin is burning, brighter and brighter, each shift of a limb screaming,

"*Watch me, watch me—watch me!*"

You finish the new routine you'll never do exactly the same again, oxygen crashing down around you triumphantly. You wait for the next song, but it never comes.

(He's gone.)

Now Playing . . .
Arial DeGroff

A major melody
to overthrow the minor
inconveniences that flood
my brain.

A tune in 4/4 time
so that 2/3 can focus
on calming down while
1/3 stumbles.

A bass line that covers
any inaccuracies a heart
pushed into overdrive.

A ballad that roars
louder than screams
muffled into worn pillows.

A waltz to accompany
the ghost of those who
never mattered in
an empty kitchen.

A quick tempo to push
heavy arms into an
erratic messy dance
with the stove as company.

A molasses tempo to
slow the never-ending
dread of future concerns.

An aria to belt out
the unfairness of
affairs committed against
an imaginary love.

A minor melody to unclog
the frog that lingers
in the throat, sipping
burning tears.

A set of lyrics that bounce
across my brain with
new promises of a
better tomorrow.

A song to help me
    feel something.

Someday
Lexus Thornton

Cold days
Cold rain
Spring has appeared once again
The pastel petals flutter in the air
As the cold winter winds disappear
Gray clouds no more
Vivid colors galore
No more masks
No more fear
This is where we'll meet again
So, I hope you'll say,
"Hi, my friend. How have you been?"
Just like time had never fled from our hands

Printed in the United States
by Baker & Taylor Publisher Services